M000307206

The Power of Respect in Business

Enabling Your Teams to Achieve Sustainable Profitable Growth

Charles Leichtweis

The Power of Respect in Business
Copyright ©2018 Charles Leichtweis

ISBN 978-1506-906-79-9 HC
ISBN 978-1506-906-62-1 PBK
ISBN 978-1506-906-63-8 EBK

LCCN 2018947617

September 2018

Published and Distributed by
First Edition Design Publishing, Inc.
P.O. Box 20217, Sarasota, FL 34276-3217
www.firsteditiondesignpublishing.com

I would like to dedicate this book to my dad. He was a lifelong educator who believed that teaching was one of the most important ways to give back.

Contents

Introduction

"Leadership is a matter of intelligence, trustworthiness, humaneness, courage, and discipline...reliance on intelligence alone results in rebelliousness. Exercise of humaneness alone results in weakness. Fixation on trust results in folly. Dependence on the strength of courage results in violence. Excessive discipline and sternness in command result in cruelty. When one has all five virtues together, each appropriate to its function, then one can be a leader." ~Sun Tzu

To me, the linchpin for operating effectively across these traits is respect. I have learned over time that leadership is an equal emphasis on respect and results. The emphasis is not 50%/50%, rather it is 100%/100%. The proof of successful leadership is in the existence of achieving both results and the relationships that make optimal results possible. A true leader knows what it means to lead and be led. Leadership does not require designated authority. Leadership can happen at all levels of an organization, and, in fact, it has to happen at all levels of the organization in order for that organization to achieve sustainable results. In order to foster that kind of culture it requires building relationships, which in turn require genuine respect. When the right relationships exist, the organization can focus like a laser on the requirements for results because it will not be running over its people to do so.

There is a good book on the subject of leadership titled *The 5 Coaching Habits of Excellent Leaders,* by Lee J. Colan, Ph.D. and Julie Davis-Colan. Dr. Colan and Julie describe the 5 coaching habits as:

1. Explain expectations. This results in alignment.
2. Ask questions. This will foster engagement.
3. Involve team. This will result in ownership.
4. Measure results. This will result in accountability.
5. Appreciate people. This will engender commitment.

The logic and practical application of these 5 habits are explained in the book in ways that provide tools to leaders and those who aspire to be great leaders. I cannot match their experience or knowledge on the subject. I would venture to add, based on my experiences, that an unsaid (perhaps obvious) element that cuts through all 5 habits is the element of respect. The application of each of the actions involved in these leadership habits does not automatically involve respect. That is not to tarnish the book or any of the points made in it. I merely believe that it is an additional dimension that relates to how these habits are implemented. That dimension requires self-awareness rooted in humility and honesty through a process of individual emotional assessment.

Respect is the linchpin of leadership. It is the secret sauce that holds all the other dimensions of leadership together in the most effective way to achieve sustainable results and sustainable profitable growth...

As I think about my journey through life and business I recall the frequent requirement, and sometimes the need, to look at results. Actual results can be measured in a number of ways; however, they are always measured against expected results. As I reflect on the moments of measuring results against expectations, one of the overriding feelings is the stress of meeting those expectations. No one, myself included, likes to feel like we have failed to meet expectations, our own or those of others. The process of measuring results is a basic step in what is known as the "management process." The management process in essence looks like:

The Management Process

Nowhere in this process does it specifically address the relationships of the people involved in the process. When we go to class to learn this process there are dozens of examples of techniques presented to measure the actual results versus the expected results and how to interpret them. Unfortunately, there is no time spent on what effect this process or what the processes performed leading up to expected/actual results has on the people involved. The result is that meaningful lessons on relationships and the role of relationships in the management/leadership process are not addressed until after the stress of the management/leadership process breaks down in ways that are detrimental to the people and organization involved.

I am what people would call an "analytical" person. I come from a line of analytical people. My father taught calculus (a complicated form of math), and my maternal grandfather was an engineer. In fact, his sons, my uncles, were engineers. Understanding what the measures of expected results should be and quantifying the key issues and concerns about the differences between expected and actual results in order to focus on corrective action comes easy for me.

I have learned over time and through some very good personal and professional advisors that the key missing ingredient from that statement is the concept of relationships

Leadership is a subject that seems to be open to interpretation in light of specific events in the business world over the last 20 years, such as the Enron scandal, the Bernie Madoff fraud, the financial crisis of 2007 due to the greed of investment banking firms such as Lehman Brothers Holdings, Inc., etc.

Leadership seems to be misunderstood on so many levels and the "success" of leadership is frequently misinterpreted when viewed through many measures of results. In a book he authored titled *Leadership*, James M. Burns described his view of the misinterpretation of leadership. He wrote:

> *"Many acts heralded or bemoaned as instances of leadership – acts of oratory, manipulation, sheer self-advancement, brute coercion – are not such. Much of what commonly passes as leadership – conspicuous position-taking without followers or follow through, posturing on various public stages, manipulation without general purpose, authoritarianism – is no more leadership than the behavior of small boys marching in front of a parade, who continue to strut along Main Street after the procession has turned down a side street toward the fairgrounds."*

As I reflect on my education in leadership I realize that, while there are specific "tools" that experts have shared to help understand the concepts of leadership, the actual lessons on leadership come from trial and error. Unfortunately, it is usually more error than success. I hope to share thoughts on some of my actual trials and errors, as well as some that I have observed and some that have been shared with me by the CEOs I interviewed for this book.

Techniques to help you do the right thing in the face of challenges can be an important way to give you a competitive advantage in dealing with difficult situations. Those techniques are usually most effective if they are simple, straight forward, and tailored to your personal situation.

What I hope you, the reader, will get out of this book is some advice, technique, or awareness of the power of respect and its application to the challenges you may face. It is not possible for us as human beings to be perfect in this area of behavior; however, if through practice we can be just 10 percent better than we are now, just think how much better our effectiveness in our relationships we would be.

I have attempted to capture lessons learned from those of us who have experienced the practical application of leadership over time. From those lessons you will be able to learn what I call the *8 secrets of achieving desired results faster:*

1. The Emotional Scale where you and others are
2. The dimensions of RESPECT
3. Listen longer/Magic moment
4. Engage with respect
5. Leadership of Respect (an equal emphasis on results and relationships)
6. SEE the HOW
7. Understanding measures of drivers and measures of results
8. Communication of judgement

By sharing these lessons I hope to accelerate the learning process for those who might not get the mentoring that would help them sooner.

Chapter 1

No One Ever Crossed the Finish Line Alone

Reaching goals is not always easy. The process has many challenges, not the least of which is developing the confidence and self-motivation to gain the necessary experience and skills for success.

Throughout our lives we try many things that are new experiences, going all the way back to the first day of kindergarten. We may have met some of our new classmates in our neighborhood, but for the most part we didn't know much about those classmates or the school procedures. In fact, we didn't even know much about ourselves. Confidence and experience are in short supply. The desire to succeed; however, is usually present. We typically find that there is at least an internal desire/need to succeed. Some may call it a competitive spirit, but the reality is that we are trying to fit it and not make mistakes. This feeling reoccurs at every stage of significant change in our lives where either we don't have the experience to feel comfortable or the confidence to deal with the issue. The risk, and therefore the fear, of failure is compounded when we are unable to assess and consider the input of all those involved.

It is the age old dilemma when a job description states that you must have experience to get the job, yet you are left wondering, "How do I get experience to get the job before I have the experience of doing the job?" The reason for looking back at these experiences in our lives is that history does repeat itself for both us and those around us.

At my age I don't remember my start in kindergarten, but I do begin to recall the issues I faced when I observe my own children. My son is six years old and in first grade. He is learning from what he sees other kids do and, more importantly, he wants to "fit in." Adults (those in positions of power) seem to know everything and are physically imposing enough that what they say can lead to fear. To a child, that fear can translate into worrying about being in trouble (punished), not getting to do something they have set their heart on (playing with friends), that they are not smart or capable of making the right decision, or that life is unfair. This can result in feeling a sense of anger, frustration, or a need to act out. To one degree or another, this cycle repeats itself at each stage of significant change in a person's life:

> Going from 8th grade to high school
> Going from high school to college
> New/Changing job
> Getting married

➢ Moving where you live
➢ Etc.

You may be wondering why I am describing the stress of change in terms of Kindergarten. As leaders, once we have gotten to where we are going it is hard to realize how we got there. When we are successful, the reflection on our personal and professional growth feels like, "I did it!" and tends to push the help and support we received from many people along the way to the background. We deal with the stress of change in different ways depending on our experience with the support we receive. This support can come in many forms and is sometimes so subtle that we don't even realize at the time that support even occurred.

Let's consider some examples. Someone you know receives a discipline report from a teacher that they have to bring home to be signed by their parents. They are afraid they are going to be in trouble and face some form of punishment. The key here is that they are afraid. They are not thinking about what happened, how to understand how it happened, or how to do better next time. The stress inside of them causes them to try to rationalize why they didn't do anything wrong, why the teacher is wrong, or why whatever "rule" they broke is not fair or stupid and should not be followed. They may even blame others. The approach you take to coach and counsel this person will have a profound impact on how that person develops their ability to learn, develop into a productive decision maker, and collaborate with others. In fact, you can negatively or positively impact the capacity of that person to lead others at whatever school or organization level they are in. If you know the person you are trying to help through this situation well, you will have a better chance at tailoring your support for them. Having a relationship with people in need of help, whether professionals or children, allows you to know where to start in helping them analyze what the learning experience means and how they can benefit from it instead of resenting it.

How many of you remember participating in a team sport? You are on a sports' team and you are trying to learn and master the right techniques of that sport (dribbling a basketball, dibbling a soccer ball, hitting a baseball, etc.) in order to be successful for yourself and your team. The coach may be frustrated that you don't understand what they are telling you about the technique. They tell you over and over again and can't understand why you don't get it! Frustration can lead to anger and perhaps things are said by the coach that don't help you perform and may even escalate the conflict. You, on the other hand, start to doubt yourself, resent how the situation makes you feel, rationalize why the coach is wrong, or all the above. If you have been in this kind of situation, it is important to recall how you felt when you are trying to help others in a similar situation.

John Lanman is CEO of a corporation in Chicago, IL. John has been a colleague of mine and I consider him a friend. He has a unique perspective regarding this example since he played college football at the University of Michigan. He described the feeling of being a part of a team from several different perspectives including what he took from those experiences:

> *"The typical football coach, always kind of the leader I respected just because I was scared shitless of him and because I never wanted to be called out and disappoint him and being*

called out for not hustling or not doing my particular job on the field right."

In that environment John felt the way any of us would have felt.

"Fear of failure is a pretty big motivator for me... The coach yells and screams and stuff like that and that's just the way football in particular would be ... I suppose because it's about getting people on board that way. Business is totally opposite. It's still a team but you can't approach the people the way a football coach might or often does, so there's a whole different management style of getting people to buy into you for other reasons. The 'kick their butt' method is not a sustainable approach. This is one of the things I learned early on, and that has made me successful and I think it comes back to building relationships"

John was referring to relationships he made with others that he could rely on for his and their mutual support and benefit.

When your coach develops a relationship with you, it helps them realize your experience and confidence levels. They can engage you on an individual basis with teachable moments. This is the best way to help you as a player with the technique you are trying to master. In addition, each player should be recognized for the success they have at their ability level. This approach will develop players at the fastest rate possible to the highest level they are capable of achieving. The next step of support is to put each player in a role that complements the team in order for them to perform at their highest level. The support for this kind of development can include people who help with physical training, nutrition advice, individual technique training, encouragement, and advice on how to overcome and solve problems.

The team example was considering how people feel when they are not in the position of power and they need to deal with the style of those who are. The other side of the coin would be someone who is already in a situation where they appear to have the position of power and control who also will respond to respect when continuing their development. Consider someone who is part of a relatively well known family who owns significant business holdings. People looking in from the outside might assume that gaining respect is not a challenge. After all, it would seem that wealth is power. I met such a person. Ashley Joyce, President, The Duchossois Family Foundation. The challenges she faced were earning respect, from both generational and gender viewpoints. When I asked Ashley how she achieved this and what she was most proud of as a leader, she said:

> *"You know, I would say it's definitely been a long process. And if I were to look at that question, and if I were to look at it towards my family and family business, I would say that I'm most proud of starting our family council. Once my generation started getting a little older, we were excited about making this a multigenerational family business. We wanted*

to know what was going on. We wanted to dig a little deeper, so I thought of a family council. I decided to kind of start that with two other cousins, and I chaired it. And it was pretty powerful, I think, especially when you had the first generation, my grandfather, who is now 95, and trying to get his respect; trying to gain my parents' and my aunts' and uncles' respect; and then my cousins, my peers. It was a little nerve wracking in the beginning, but I'm happy to say it's very successful. I've passed the baton to one of my other cousins after seven years, and it's still thriving and doing well, and it's very organized, and the family, I really think, has respected it."

The chairman of the board of the family holdings encouraged, supported, and validated her ability even though they didn't always agree.

"It's nice to have that validation. When someone says Ashley, you know what? Here is what we see in you. Even though I'm a pretty confident person, it still is really nice."

Respecting and encouraging others to develop themselves as leaders, just as she had experienced in her life, is an idea that Ashley has carried forward in her successful career running corporations and serving on boards.

I also interviewed Jamie Johnson, the CEO of Verde Sustainable Solutions, who wanted to use his passion to start a company that specialized in identifying and installing environmental friendly lighting specifications. He left his job as a firefighter after 10 years to pursue this passion. He spoke about support and respect from two perspectives. One, how they played a role in his development, and two, of how to show respect to build a team that would help him realize his goals.

Jamie fist relayed a story from the firehouse:

> *"So, at the fire house I had a lieutenant who now is the fire chief there and when I started the first day he threw a tank on his back with me and we did stairs, like he was right there in the beginning teaching me what was important, role modeling really, and I think I valued that. It spoke to me, made me feel welcome and cared about and I think that is why he is chief now because he did that."*

Jamie was able to translate the result of what he learned from the respect he was shown by his lieutenant into building a team that would help him turn his entrepreneurial dream into a reality. When I asked him how he engaged in the challenge of training people while learning at the same time, he replied:

> *"It was slow, you know, we're boot strapped so I mean there's been no injection of capital but at the same time we're able to…double every year… which is great but it's a long year, maybe we add two or three people over the year, so we add them, we train them, get them about three months to get up to speed…"*

In addition to investing in their training, he went on to say:

> *"I'm very forgiving of mistakes because I make a lot of mistakes myself, as long as someone just admits that it was a mistake. I have a hard time if someone is not willing to say guys I screwed up. I have a level of trust with them that exceeds this role as employer."*

So far we have described examples of a situation involving a person who is beginning to learn what life is about, a sports team involving the development of individual members along with the whole team, a young talented woman's career development, and an entrepreneur striving to follow his passion and provide for his new family. Now let's talk about one more example involving me.

This example is a goal I sought to accomplish. The goal was one I had never achieved in my life, in fact, I had never even attempted it. At 60 years old I definitely had to step outside my comfort zone. The goal by any estimates would take a significant commitment of time with significant perseverance and endurance.

I had an important goal to "cross the finish line" in 2013 and I committed to doing it with my oldest daughter. The goal required significant effort over a period of more than a year in preparation for merely completing the goal, not to mention doing well compared to others. Training to run 26.2 miles involves progressive, grueling steps that will certainly create pain, self-doubt, pride, elation, set-backs, and progress on a roller coaster of events in an attempt to realize success. Sound familiar? You may have never trained to run a 26.2 mile marathon; however, I would bet the process I just described is similar to the roller coaster of emotions we experience in successfully leading organizations.

Now let's think about a running a marathon. Most people look at this as a purely individual event with individual accomplishment. If I was standing on a street corner and you asked people passing by about what a marathon runner would look like, I am clearly not the prototype for what one thinks of as a marathon runner. I don't consider myself out of shape; however, I am 6 feet 2 inches, 230 pounds, and I had never run farther than 12 miles in my life, let alone 26.2 miles! In my training I quickly realized that there is a reason the typical marathon runner is not 230 pounds. In any event, I had a goal to run a marathon with my 24 year old daughter. In order to attempt this goal, I needed to believe that I could do this. I planned to run the 2013 Chicago Marathon!

In talking with folks at "running" stores and reading various published training materials, I was able to understand that people of all ages, shapes, and sizes have been able to realize this goal. Still, the respect I received from the experienced runners who worked at the fitness stores and centers I visited was very rewarding and motivating to me. Their respect and encouragement, even though I was nowhere near their level in the sport, began to help me trust in myself to do this. I trained, sometimes in frustration and pain, but with the belief that I could accomplish my goal. Along the way, I could not have accomplished this without encouragement from my family, experts in marathons, and nutritionists, among many others. As a result, I was able to break my goal down into logical, understandable terms to help me focus on being successful within my ability and within the magnitude of the event. My goal was simply to "cross the finish line, and do it standing up"—and I did it!

How do these examples relate to the "no one crossed the finish line alone" analogy? The examples I have provided demonstrate that there are many elements of person's experience and support that have a bearing on the level and sustainability of accomplishing goals, whether as a team or as individuals within the team.

Trust is a key element of human relationships, yet it is only a subset of a more comprehensive picture of being a leader and helping people cross their finish line. To me, that more comprehensive picture of the *Leadership of Respect* involves:

> **R**ecognition/listening
> **E**ncouragement/empathy/ethics
> **S**upport/sincerity/servant leadership
> **P**ractice/patience
> **E**xperience/sharing/honesty
> **C**oaching/communication/caring
> **T**rust/transparency/training

In a perfect world we would probably be able to say the message here is obvious. However, we don't live in a perfect world, and there are so many pressures and distractions that it is very difficult to reflect on our experiences to help us understand how to most effectively lead others. Each person's development needs may require an individual approach to respect. To be the most effective leader you must seek to understand those different approaches and act accordingly.

Demonstrating respect and all it involves per the elements identified above, requires the ability to listen when you may not appreciate the communication style of the people who you work with. It requires encouragement when you may not agree with the timing of results being achieved. It requires coaching and sincerity when you don't see the expected results being achieved. It requires empathy, honesty, and transparency when people make mistakes in executing key processes. It requires practice and training when your associates don't initially understand the objectives of the organization or their particular role in achieving results. Finally, it requires sharing and recognition when even small examples of success towards achieving results happen in your organization.

You will notice that respect does not avoid an emphasis on results. True leadership involves an equal emphasis on results *and* relationships. It is not an emphasis of 50%/50%. It needs to be an emphasis of 100%/100%. When we built trust with the union at a manufacturing company through the **Leadership of Respect** we found that focusing the business on service levels, productivity, and margin improvement was accepted by the union members. This collaborative effort led to more than doubling productivity and service levels, as well as a 15% improvement in margins as a percentage of sales. The increase in service levels to meet customer and channel requirements in turn allowed for increased penetration of existing customers in addition to penetrating new customers. The ultimate result was a double digit compound growth rate over a four year period.

Continuous improvement requires continuous respect.

This attitude and respect needs to be from top to bottom in an organization. Communication style and content from the leadership demonstrate the commitment to respect or not. I have found over my career that the steps in the communication process to create a success driven culture and a culture of continuous improvement must include at least the following:

- ✓ Transparent sharing of the objectives for the organization
- ✓ Define what success looks like in terms of results
- ✓ Engaging the associates in the process of identifying barriers to achieve expected results
- ✓ Engaging associates in the process of overcoming barriers to achieve expected results
- ✓ Publish results against the objectives to all associates
- ✓ Establish and communicate recognition and reward systems for achieving expected results and achieving successes in improving processes that result in achieving expected results

Titus Plautus, a Roman playwright, wrote, "No man is wise enough by himself." Johann Wolfgang von Goethe, German writer and statesman, put it this way: "Treat people as if they were what they ought to be and help them to become what they are capable of being."

As you reflect on who helped you cross each of the finish lines that have challenged you in your career, keep in mind how that helped you and how you can help others. Even if you feel that people only worked against your development, remember how that feels and hopefully that will inspire you not to create in others the cycle of frustration, resentment, and perhaps anger you may have felt. Always strive to show respect to others—your return on that investment will be exponential.

When you help someone believe in themselves, they will set bigger goals.

Chapter 2

Don't Ride Your Bike with
Your Mouth Open

When was the last time you rode your bicycle? Depending on the weather where you live, it may have been in the summer time, or at least when it was warm enough outside to be comfortable. You might have to dig deep in your memory to remember when you last rode, so perhaps I can help you recall the experience.

It's a clear day and you are moving along smoothly, at a reasonable speed, taking in the scenery. You have done this many times before, even if the last time was when you were a kid. The path you are on is very familiar. While I'm sure you enjoy riding in the sun, there are some shaded and perhaps wooded areas on the path.

While there is nothing in your face in the sunny open air, when you reach the shaded or wooded areas there are bugs flying and sometimes tree debris hanging down from branches. As you approach these areas you are aware of these potential obstacles, but you don't know when and where they will be. Undoubtedly you don't want to get bugs or other debris in your mouth. No one would. Since the details of the situation are unknown, the best thing to do is consciously close your mouth to prevent making the mistake of opening your mouth and swallowing bugs or debris. The chance of making this mistake is exacerbated by the rapidly changing condition of the environment. To be most successful in your objective of managing and mitigating problems, you need to be prepared for an unknown and rapidly changing environment. In other words, if you don't want to catch unwanted bugs and debris, **don't ride your bike with your mouth open!**

The same principal applies to leadership and your ability to create and manage relationships that are required for leading people to achieve objectives. When you join in the discussion of issues in your business, the environment may be as unknown and rapidly changing as the bike path you were on when you entered the wooded area of the path. The "environment" I am referring to is the experience of those charged with managing an area of your business, their emotional state (where they are coming from) at the time of conversation, and the facts of the problem or situation that may have changed since you were last informed. It is important to realize that the environment can have unknown and constantly changing factors like those on your bike path. The best way to prevent interrupting the enjoyable journey of effectively leading and motivating others (also known as inadvertently swallowing bugs) is to keep in mind the advice **"don't ride your bike with your**

mouth open!"

Let's take a look at an example of what happens if we don't realize the environment we are in when we attempt to manage a problem to effectively achieve an objective.

The landscaping example: Our neighbor has a nice yard at their house. Nothing fancy or unusual, just a nice yard with some flower gardens. I have rarely seen them working on or in their yard. Occasionally they will cut the grass when needed, but with high school age kids I think their priorities are elsewhere. He is constantly training for triathlons and with the exception of sun bathing, she is rarely in the yard. They are busy with things other than their yard.

Our yard, on the other hand, is something we get great enjoyment from. We have landscaped it significantly with plants of all kinds and we take great pride in maintaining it even though we are also very busy and have small children who need our attention. I grew up working for my dad in landscaping since I was 10 years old. My wife is very knowledgeable about gardens and flower/shrub landscapes, as her mother is a master gardener with the Chicago Botanical gardens, and the apple doesn't fall far from the tree...no pun intended.

Our neighbor chose a landscaping company to clean up the leaves in the fall. When cleaning up the leaves, the company left a bunch of leaf material in the street. The leaves built up along the curb and began to bleed down the street a little at a time when it rained, creating a mess in front of several houses including ours. I was frustrated by this because it was important to me to clean up this type of material and it meant I would be cleaning up a mess for some time as it ran down the street. I thought this was very inconsiderate of our neighbor and their landscaping company. I thought about talking to our neighbor and asking him to have the street in front of their house cleaned up.

I thought of several ways to ask them and realized that the request would come out in a negative way due to my frustration. I decided to wait until I saw him casually over the fence in the backyard and maybe talk about how the leaves are falling late this year. Coincidently, that's exactly what happened a day or so later. He started to talk about leaves falling late and how he would have his service come again to clean up all the leaves that had finally fallen since the last clean up. I seized the opportunity to say "you might want to mention to your service that they should also clean up the street in front." His reply was, "Are there a lot of leaves in the street?" This seemed incredible to me, because there was a big mess in the street in my opinion. I said yes and he said ok. As I thought about his reply, it dawned on me that the street or leaves in it did not even register on his mental radar. The fact that his perspective on how he thought of yards or gardens or leaves was so different from my perspective is how and why it didn't register with him.

Fortunately in this case I didn't get in his face about it. Goodness knows I wanted to give someone a piece of my mind for what I thought was an obvious form of being inconsiderate. If I had recognized the signs of his yard and how they chose to use it versus our yard and how we chose to use it, I would have realized in advance that the situation was not what I felt it was. Even though I did not appreciate our neighbors' lack of attention to detail, the action was not the result of not caring about us. I could have saved myself the frustration and potential conflict of a negative personal interaction had I taken the time to really assess the situation when I first felt frustrated by it.

The story I have just told is a lesson in avoiding conflict by not escalating a situation until reflecting on all aspects of it. This story actually has more to it, unfortunately a less positive side.

About two weeks later, our neighbor's landscaping service came to pick up the leaves in their yard. Our gardens border the property line between the two houses. The last time they used a powerful blower on wheels to clear a small section of land approximately 4 feet wide and 25 feet long next to the our gardens, they ended up breaking some of the plants and spreading leaves back onto our clean lawn. I said nothing to them and simply picked up the debris myself. This time; however, they were taking the same action while I was home. I went out to ask them to turn off the blower, which was obviously the wrong tool for the space as it was creating the same problem as before. The crew member would not turn it off and our conversation was loud due to the very loud machine. I finally understood that he said I needed to talk to his boss, who was the person in our neighbors' backyard, and that he wouldn't turn off the big blower. I reached out to the boss by shouting "hey" twice, but he couldn't hear me because he was also operating a back pack blower. My frustration was building again based on my thoughts from their previous visit, what was going on now, and how they didn't appear to be willing to stop and listen. As I got closer to the boss I shouted "HEY" very loudly. I startled him so much that he literally jumped up in the air as he turned around. My feeling of being disrespected was so high that I continued to shout even after he turned off his machine. I yelled at him to stop using the big machine in and near our garden and that they better pick up the debris that they were blowing.

You'll never guess what he said to me. He said, "Do you want me to respect you?" That's really what he said! I replied yes and he said, "Then respect me by not yelling at me." At that point he said he would use his machines to get the debris off our lawn and walked away. I felt bad and was still frustrated because they proceeded to drag their big machine through our garden, damaging plants while they blew the leaves off our lawn. I was unable to affect the situation effectively. By letting my frustration escalate, I was no longer able to communicate what I needed in a way that would bring the desired result. I should have more sufficiently communicated that they not use the big machine for the small area next to our garden and that, instead, they should use a rake, which would have prevented the extra debris and damage to our plants.

The Emotional Scale

I believe the landscaping example illustrates the point that there is what I would call the **Emotional Scale:**

The Emotional Scale is a scale of how we feel when someone or something interacts with us. The scale applies not only for ourselves, but for the people we are interacting with. This can progress up or down through the feelings described:

> **Happy** (This is when you are feeling valued.)

> **Disappointment** (This could be feelings of disappointment in yourself or in others based on feedback.)

➤ **Frustration** (This is a normal feeling and a point that you can begin to control what happens next with your emotions.......or not.)

➤ **Realization of need to improve** (This will likely occur based on the environment in which you work, the amount of constructive direction you receive, and the amount of respect you are counseled on.)

➤ **Unfairly treated** (This is a tipping point for many people to moving up the scale. Your personal sense of fairness is a key learning factor that can be a powerful tool to manage your next reaction and the reaction of others to conflict.)

➤ **Anger** (This can be normal when feeling disrespected. It is an emotion that you should let yourself feel and try to let subside, over time if necessary, before you react. The key is to find a diversion to these feelings and not let them consume you.)

➤ **Insulted** (This feeling can cause people to enter the difficult stage of personal worth which, in turn, could result in feelings of getting even (revenge) or shutting down completely. Either way, you don't want to push people to this stage of emotion or let yourself go here.)

➤ **Revenge** (It is hard to turn back from this feeling.)

➤ **Violence** (This is the point of no return.)

Where you are on this scale at any point in time can seriously affect your ability to be effective, motivate others, and achieve your desired results.

Both parties involved in a confrontation where one disrespects the other will usually feel bad afterwards; however, they may feel bad for different reasons. The person being disrespected will obviously feel bad for how they were treated and may even be convinced to feel bad about their ability because of how their confidence may have been destroyed. The person who disrespected the other will feel bad in some cases because of the effect they had on the person they disrespected, because they lost control of themselves, or because they are feeling one of the emotions on the scale defined above. It is true that when something goes wrong the person with the expectation of performance can be as disappointed, frustrated, or angry because performance goals were not met.

They secret here is to learn two critically important things about the scale:

1. Where you and others are on the scale at any moment
2. What triggers you and others to move up or down the scale

I'm not suggesting you become consumed with thinking about where you are on the scale to the exclusion of focusing on what you are supposed to be doing. However, I do believe that an occasional realization of where you are on the scale will help you learn what triggers you to move up or down on the scale.

What triggers you to move on the scale is one of the

most important self-awareness levels you can reach. If you spend some time reflecting on what was going on and what you felt when you are in some of the more ineffective levels of the Emotional Scale, you will discover characteristics about yourself and others that affect your reactions. The next step is to develop a "trigger" for yourself to help you manage when and how much you move on the scale. It is important to recognize that as human beings we all can move up and down the scale every day. It is not a problem that we can move on the scale. It is very important that we learn to control how much we should move and when. Since I am addressing techniques that involve leadership in business, I am not addressing nor advocating the violence level on the scale.

Picture yourself in a high pressure situation where sales growth is critical to meeting your performance goals. You enter a meeting to review new product development timetables with a lot of optimism in the belief that your customers and sales organization have expressed their excitement and belief in the product concepts. As the meeting unfolds you begin to find out that timetables for the process from concept to market execution are not being met. You begin to move up the Emotional Scale from happy to disappointment. As the discussion continues you are now entering the on ramp to the frustration highway! You may not realize it, but what you do next will set up how your team will:

- ✓ Develop confidence to do their job
- ✓ Learn to react to adversity
- ✓ Be motivated to learn how to trouble shoot problems

Regardless of the cause for delays in the timeline, all of these learnings/experiences by your team are critical for them to be able to manage themselves to create sustainable profitable growth. Just as in the story about the landscaping incident, the business situation described here has implications on when, why, and how you travel up or down the Emotional Scale. With that in mind, hindsight suggests that you should realize the following when you hear about the delays that are negatively affecting your business:

> ➢ Anger in the current meeting will not accomplish the objective of discovering the problem and creating a plan to fix it.
> ➢ Yelling at folks will cause them to shut down and react with anger or frustration or both in return.

Let me be clear, it is normal to feel frustration and even anger when confronted with problems. It does not make us bad people. When you reflect on what likely upsets you, you can then begin to recognize those situations in advance. The secret is to develop your own personal trigger to think about when you see those situations/people coming. What I mean by "trigger" here is a "word" that you can recall in your mind that causes you to pause before reacting verbally or through body language. For me my trigger word is "Respect." I'm sure that comes to you as no surprise given the title of this book.

How it works is that as you encounter a situation that sets you off, you think about your trigger word. When I see those situations coming (not always) I have learned to think to myself, "How can I respect the people involved?" When I am successful in doing this, I find that several things happen:

- ➤ I pause enough before moving up the Emotional Scale™ and, therefore, mitigate the possibility of that movement clouding my ability to lead.
- ➤ I begin to think more clearly about problem solutions instead of just problem causes.
- ➤ I more clearly come up with direction to the people involved that might be helpful to them.
- ➤ I engage the people needed to help identify the causes and solve the problem instead of shutting them down.
- ➤ I get the information necessary to timely communicate to all affected parties (other functions, appropriate management, customers, suppliers, etc.) in a way that allows for the support for a successful solution to the problem no matter how difficult.

Practice

Did you ever notice during your career that describing and analyzing a difficult situation after the fact is infinitely easier that managing in the middle of the turmoil? Have you ever been on a sports team during a big game, had to give a music recital, perform in a play, or give a really important speech/presentation that could determine the path of your career?

Try to remember what it was like. You felt apprehension, excitement, anticipation, confidence, maybe even self-doubt. Your goal is to perform flawlessly when the pressure of the moment is on! How do you prepare for the "moment of truth" when you have to react instinctively in an instant with all eyes upon you? The answer that is consistent across all of those situations is…..PRACTICE. In spite of what Alvin Iverson of the Philadelphia 76ers contends, practice is very important to perform to the best of our ability in key situations. This is true of leadership as well. Practicing leadership will put you in the position of superior performance in challenging times as well as less challenging times. Are there any "less challenging times" these days?

In any event, practicing to learn where we are on the Emotional Scale and what triggers our movement up and down the scale will help us to perform at our best in all situations in business and in life. In addition, practicing to learn where others are on the scale and what triggers their movement up and down the scale will equally help us to perform at our best. It is important to keep in mind that how we act/react will in fact cause others to be at a certain place on the scale as well as trigger their movement. This is a key point in being able to develop the relationships necessary to lead.

Another element of leadership to focus on in these situations goes hand in hand with developing your own personal trigger to being more effective. That element is **communication**. After you have put yourself in a position to be more successful in the face of adversity, how you begin to communicate is equally important. Remember the discussion about riding your bike with your mouth open? When you do that you are likely to eat some bugs! Like the unknown and constantly changing environment of the wooded area on the bike path, if you enter a situation you are supposed to lead with your mouth open, you are likely to experience the equivalent of eating bugs, such as:

> ➢ Alienating those people you need the most to help the situation get resolved
> ➢ Misunderstanding the facts of a situation and setting the wrong direction for the business
> ➢ Causing people in your organization to stop speaking up in the future

If a person asked you to come around the corner of a building to see you and when they did you punched them in the mouth, do you think that person would come around the corner the next time you asked them? Would you if that happened to you? This is what happens if people's ideas are constantly shut down in a conversation about a problem that is being discussed.

I believe that leadership is an equal emphasis on results and relationships. It's not 50/50, it's 100/100. I have forgotten where I learned that, but it is a very important concept that we should all learn how to manage. As I stated in the forward to this book, I am an analytical person. As an analytical person, my ability to understand and focus on results comes easily. For me, the other main point of emphasis for leadership, relationships, takes effort and requires a learning curve with plenty of practice. The type of practice that I received the most was originally from experiencing the reaction people had to me and my style of focusing on results. I can tell you that at times those reactions weren't pretty. The type of practice I eventually benefited most from was understanding the Emotional Scale and how to identify my trigger for moving up or down the scale.

As I mentioned, communication plays an important role as we develop our leadership ability. What I am referring to here is how we engage people even when we are cognizant of the scale.

Analytical people, myself included, sometimes have the ability to quickly see the steps for how a problem needs to be solved, or at least we think we do!

When you are in a meeting with one or more people from your organization, and the conversation gets bogged down on discussing the problem and/or possible solutions, do you feel you see the path to the solution? Do you want the group to move along much faster on their task because there is so much to be done and you have resource constraints? It's hard not to feel that way. The problem with interjecting your thoughts too fast to the group is that you risk losing them and the benefit of their ideas to help this and future problems.

A good friend and colleague of mine, John Cassin a former CHRO and General Manager, once gave me some life altering advice. For me, when I "see" the solution to a problem that others are needed to solve, I tend to move to that "aha" moment too fast. I believe I know where the group should go and I start leading them there. We analytical folks are good at that. However, even if we "see" the correct solution, our style of focusing the group to a solution they don't yet see will have unintended negative consequences. While I didn't realize what the problem was with this approach, I sensed something was not working with some of the teams I was supposed to lead.

John is the most skilled person I have ever met at diagnosing relationship issues. And make no mistake, the example of "seeing" a solution too fast can cause relationship issues, and relationship issues will cause results issues! The advice he gave me was to "listen longer." These two simple words can be easy to remember if we are not in the wrong place on the Emotional Scale. In my experience, the brilliance of those two words will result in:

➢ The person you are listening to will feel that you are really listening.
➢ When you let someone take the time to clearly articulate their issue you may find that the issue that needs resolution may be very different from the one you originally diagnosed.
➢ The person you are listening to feels respected and you will be able to build the trust and confidence that gives that person the chance to perform at the highest level they are capable of.
➢ You will be much more effective at motivating people and achieving results.

Robert Jordan, former news anchor and Journalist for WGN in Chicago, described an example of the second point above. He described this in the context of being a reporter interviewing people who were not used to speaking into a microphone in front of a camera. He said when you are a young reporter and you are set to interview someone it is important to recognize that they may have fears/anxiety that come about in the interview situation.

> *"I think one of the most important areas for gaining respect and appreciation is to listen carefully. There's something called a golden moment that inexperienced reporters don't know about, or haven't learned about. The golden moment occurs during a conversation,*

*when you ask someone a question, they will blurt out an answer, and they're finished. So if you jump right in, right away, and ask another question, you've missed the golden moment. When you sit there and listen, many times there's this awkward silence and the interviewee will then get right back into it and give you a summary answer, and that's what the **golden moment** has achieved. When you listen to people talk and give them an opportunity to move through the golden moment, you're going to get a great answer. People appreciate it. Now they've summed up what it was they were trying to say. You've gotten the best of what it is that you're looking for...but, if you jump right in some times and don't, you're so busy trying to blah, blah, blah, badgering somebody."*

Robert also noted another helpful technique when communicating with people:

"Something else happens when you listen carefully to people. It puts them at ease, and people tell me all the time during an interview, at the beginning you can sense they're nervous. You can hear their mouths are dry and they might fidget. So, I will usually, while the camera crew is setting up, carry on what we call a pre-interview interview. I'll talk to them, maybe about their grand kids, or, I'll say, man, I like that tie, or a woman, where'd you get

those earrings, my wife would love those earrings. You just put someone really at ease just by saying that. Just by that, where did you get that tie?"

A practical example of listening longer comes from a story in a book titled **Among Friends: Stories from the Journey** by Father John Sichko. He wrote:

> *"As I entered the kindergarten class, the children sat on a rug while the teacher taught them about colors. They invited me to participate and I asked the kids, Can you tell me what color apples are?*
>
> *Hands shot to the sky." Father John says "One thing I've learned is that you never want to call on the first person who raises their hand. In this situation, a little boy named David bounced up and down to get my attention....So, to avoid that conversation, I called on a little girl who answered, "Apples are red."*
>
> *Father John said "Yes, that's true, that's correct. Apples are red." He goes on to say "Another boy answered and said, "Apples are green." John said "That's also correct."*
>
> *He then describes "another girl raised her hand and answered, "Sometimes apples are yellow." To which he wrote "I agreed with the girl, but, again little David waved his hand, insisting to be recognized. I sighed and said, "Alright, David. What color are apples?*

He said "Father, apples are white!"

All the little kids giggled.

Father John replied "Uh, David, I don't believe I've ever seen a white apple" He wrote "I didn't want to make the kid feel stupid in front of his friends, so I adopted my "fake" thoughtful look."

Before he could move on, David stood up and said "Father, haven't you ever bitten into an apple before? It's white on the inside."

Everyone got quiet, and John said, "David, you're right. Apples are white." Father John concluded "We all just need to look a little deeper."

"Looking a little deeper" includes "listening a little longer" and taking the time to talk to people you may not want to talk to. It also means giving them the respect that allows them to get their ideas on the table so that everyone can be potentially enlightened by thoughts that otherwise would never be brought forward. In this story these concepts work even for a priest, a teacher we presume to follow the principles of respect and openness to others. I can tell you with certainty it has worked for me.

The advice of John Cassin, Father John Schiko, and Robert Jordan are examples of great life lessons that will make any of us more effective leaders.

Chapter 3

Engage with Respect

Communication (written, verbal, and non-verbal) is how we affect the actions and attitudes of others, which in turn have a significant impact on the success of an organization. In all organizations there are at least two paths of communication: formal and informal. The formal path is done in accordance with the rules of convention or etiquette and usually represents the sanctioned position of the topic communicated. The phrase "keep on message" comes to mind. The informal path is more casual and, quite frankly, not always in accordance with the rules of convention and etiquette. What percentage of each type of communication is found in your organization? In a typical organization, George De Mare stated that as much as 70% of all communication is through the informal path.

There are many articles published about the goal of

communication from the point of view of the sender and receiver of formal communication. Those collective articles point out that the goal of communication is to promote complete understanding of a message and that there are some emotional and environmental obstacles that prevent effective communication.

I interviewed John Cassin, CEO of JDC solutions and one of the most aware people with respect to the feelings and motivation of others that I have met in business. In that interview I asked him what was his most effective communication strategies are and why he felt they were successful. His main point in response was that he "found one-on-one communication to be the most effective means of being able to communicate effectively." He went on to say "while communicating with individuals or groups it is most important not to be judgmental". As I reflected on John's words, I personally feel that it can be difficult to not appear judgmental, even if it is not your intention to judge someone else. I can think of many times that I have thought "I don't like that" or "that does not make sense to me." When that happens and I am not concentrating on my response, or if I have not prepared myself enough with how I should respond, there is a good chance I might make a face or other body language that communicates my judgement of the situation. This in turn communicates to the person or persons I am speaking with that I am judging them unfavorably when that is not my intention or the right thing to do as a leader. It takes practice to master the skill of active listening and not being judgmental.

It may be helpful to think about how we feel when someone interrupts us. Thinking about it from the point of view of the person trying to explain their thoughts will allow us to realize that interrupting can make people feel like you are just not interested in what they have to say or make them feel that you think that what you have to say is more important. It might help to keep in mind that if you are right now, you will be right later. Listen first.

How do you work on the skill of active listening and avoiding treating people in a judgmental manner? John Cassin says the answer is to practice these skills by talking with people you don't agree with. In doing so, listen carefully and don't react to what they are saying. When necessary, ask for clarification on their thinking to understand where they are coming from. Do not think of the discussion as one in which you need to get your point across. In the best case scenario you might gain an understanding of the other person(s) that is helpful for your ability to engage and lead them. In the worst case scenario you will have shown your ability to listen and move on without creating unnecessary conflict. You will, in fact, have acted in a way that builds trust by showing respect. There is another age old saying that expresses this: "seek to understand before being understood." When you practice by talking with someone you don't agree with you work on not reacting to what they are saying. By listening longer you can practice verbal and non-verbal reactions and at the same time improve your relationship with that person(s).

I had a conversation about this concept with a colleague of mine and his concern was, "Does this mean that you have to listen to the person and you never get to make your own point?" I replied that as you listen actively to what you may not agree with several things will happen that will inform you how to make your response. First, you will gain the best understanding of what specifically you disagree with.

Second, you will also gain an understanding of what part of the issue you might agree with. Third, because of the first and second points, you will be in a position to better present your point of view in light of potential common ground and the reasons that formed your opinion without belittling the other person's point of view. The result may be an agreement to disagree; however, there will not be the disrespect involved in disagreements that cause frustration, resentment, and anger that prevent organizations from achieving desired results. The encounter may reveal that someone is expected to perform in a way that they are not ready for and that the person not ready to perform may need another position, but it will less likely be a surprise. Even though changing a person's position (including an exit) is hard for the organization, the remaining associates will be able to realize that respect and fairness were part of the process. That realization will allow the organization to move forward in a positive direction.

Informal methods of communication, such as rumors and "the company grapevine," can be outside of management's control. In the absence of access to communication among all associates, including management, some associates will put forth their version of the truth based on how they feel about what is happening at the company. Although there is no way the grapevine can be stopped, it can be influenced. In fact, the goal in an organization should be to appropriately influence the grapevine, not to eliminate it.

A company with a globally recognized brand was struggling with everything from results to relationships. The existing CEO was exited and the head of operations was tagged to run the business in the interim. Eventually I was brought in to be the CEO to help turn around this neglected company that was on the brink of bankruptcy. The company was a cash drain, losing money with a balance sheet that was overrun with inventory levels equal to the company's sales. Half of the inventory was made up of product not currently being sold. In addition, a classic labor/management dispute was holding back both productivity and the ability to service customers. You might be wondering why anyone would take on this challenge. Sounds pretty dire. On the bright side, the company had the number one aided or unaided brand recognition in its category, retailers knew consumers had/would buy significant amounts of the company's product if they could keep it on their shelves, and the associates really did want the company to do well (their jobs relied on it!) if they could get effective leadership. In learning the business I noted that their strategy was wrong given the core competencies of the business, and because of this, the key business processes were not aligned to support a strategy that would result in sustainable profitable growth.

You may recognize one or more of the problems that this company faced in your organization. Hopefully more of the positive elements and not all of the challenges at once! There are many root causes to these problems that have to be uncovered, prioritized, and remediated. Where do you suppose a CEO should start? Should there be a demand for accountability or a search for the root causes based on existing inaccurate data and measurements? No, I started with communication!

I mentioned a labor/management dispute. There was a well-recognized national union representing the factory associates. Historically, management practiced a control and command approach to communication – share nothing and control all information. The natural conflict between the two groups was a classic "us versus them" that created an opportunity for the informal organization to perpetuate the message of mutual distrust and lack of common purpose.

The Parable of the Three Stonecutters:

Once upon a time, a traveler came across three stonecutters and asked them what they were doing.

The first replied that he was the most miserable person on Earth and that he had the hardest job in the world. "Every day I have to move around huge stones to make a living, which is barely enough to eat." The traveler gave him a coin and continued on.

The second stonecutter did not complain and was focused on his work. When the traveler asked him what he was doing, the stonecutter replied, "I am earning a living by doing the best job of stonecutting in the entire country. Although the work is hard, I'm satisfied with what I do and I earn enough money to feed my family." The traveler praised him, gave him a coin, and went on.

When the traveler met the third stonecutter, he noticed that the stonecutter had sweat and dust on him but he looked very happy and was singing a cheerful song. The traveler was astonished and asked, "What are you doing?" The stonecutter looked up with a visionary

gleam in his eye and said, "Can't you see? I am building a cathedral."
(*The Practice of Management* Peter F Drucker 1954*)*

Some people may naturally have the vision and understanding of the impact what they do at work has, as well as the attitude to embrace that role. I believe that there are many more people who could learn to embrace their role the way the third stonecutter did if they are engaged in the ways described in this book....with respect. I believe at the heart of it all is respect. Without respect and the underlying communication of support and trust that goes with it, the risk of empowerment is too high and the barriers to engagement are too great.

Regarding the company I described above, one of the first steps put into practice was daily encounters with the factory personnel by walking through the factory, greeting each person, learning their names, and what their jobs were. By becoming visible to the formal and informal organization, I began to demonstrate respect for them and what they do for a living. We began to build mutual respect, which led to their trust in my leadership.

A second major step was setting up quarterly "all company" meetings. Quarterly all company meetings included all associates and provided a forum for communication with the entire company present. The meetings were organized in two 45 minute sections. The first section of the meeting was designed to have sales and marketing communicate their efforts to grow the business. This had the effect of letting people understand the hope for the future that was needed for all to be engaged in "building the cathedral." The second half of the meeting was designed to allow anyone present to raise any issue or concern they felt the need to address. During the second half of the first meeting you would have thought a riot was going to break out! People were shouting at each other claiming that they were not getting the necessary help from each other or management. The senior leadership team that I inherited remarked after the meeting, "We better not have another one of those meetings!" and "people were out of control in there."

I smiled and said, "Because of what happened in there, we absolutely need to have more of those meetings." During the meeting I told the associates that everyone there had the right to ask questions and to get answers. It was also pointed out that they might not always like the answers, but this was how we needed to operate, starting at the departmental level in the company. This was the beginning of building a relationship anchored in respect and resulting in the support and trust to move the organization forward. It also began to shed more light on the actions needed to address those issues in the company, which began to mitigate any inaccurate or destructive information that circulated through the informal organization. A key point of what I am describing here is engaging the associates of the company, not empowering them to make all the decisions on their own. I believe there is a big difference. It is the difference between leadership and abdication of responsibility.

Another event that occurred shortly after the first all company meeting was a meeting with the union committee. The union insisted on the meeting. Although a meeting between the union committee and the CEO was not normal protocol, the directors of operations and human resources agreed with the idea, so the meeting was set. The three members of the union committee filed in the small conference room above the manufacturing floor. After being seated, the committee members stated that they had one question for the new CEO: "What do you think of unions?"

I replied: "I don't. We are here to create sustainable jobs at the company, and to do that we need to be competitive, profitable, and flexible." I also said, "I look out at the manufacturing floor and I don't see union or non-union employees, I see people who need jobs to support their families." I then turned to the union committee and said in all honesty, "I don't know about you, but I need this job!" Several important points were made in this conversation. One was the need for flexibility, to allow the company to react to market pressures. Another was to put the focus of threats to the company on competition in the market place. A third major point was the common need for the jobs they all have and that this was a common interest that bonds both sides in a way that didn't exist before. The need to communicate and begin the bonding process was accomplished with the backdrop of a relationship based on respect.

The result of demonstrating respect and building trust that fostered a belief in a common purpose, shared goals, and accountability led to:

> ➤ A ground breaking contract with a nationally known union that allowed the organization to focus on service levels, productivity, safety, quality, and profitability for everyone's benefit.
> ➤ An improvement in service levels from 47% to 98.5%.

➤ An improvement in productivity from 40% to 85%
➤ Reversal of a rapidly declining top line. Organic net sales growth at a compound growth rate of 5% over the last four years versus a compounded loss of sales of 14% for the previous three years.
➤ Significant active SKU reduction (by 19%, from 8,000 to 6,500), and channel/product optimization.
➤ A breakeven point lowered by 15% while growing the top line and funding key investment in the business through growth.
➤ Increased cash flow by discontinuing unprofitable lines and lowering inventory investment by 50%.
➤ Improved productivity through focused engagement of employees at all levels of the manufacturing process.

The stories above laid a foundation of respect which in turn created a foundation for a common focus on improving the business. Beyond the foundation of these critical elements is the ongoing role of communication. Communication is an area that has its own set of challenges since the dawn of time. One of the most significant challenges is that no two people are exactly the same. In order to be most effective in communication we somehow need to recognize the differences in both the sender and receiver. All of our experiences and natural emotional makeup enter into how we react to the communication process. The reality of pressure, time, or performance exacerbates the complication of the communication process. Learning where we are on the Emotional Scale described in this book, as well what triggers a movement up or down the scale, is a practical way to think about where the sender and receiver are in a conversation and how they might react to the issues discussed.

Remembering your journey over your career can provide lessons in hindsight about where you place on the Emotional Scale and how you reacted to the circumstances you encountered. Everyone's career journey involves a variety of roles and responsibilities. Each role adds to your experience and confidence to aspire to a broader role with more responsibilities. In each step on your journey you learn and utilize the skills that you are best at. Some people are good at qualitative skills, others are good at quantitative skills, and some have skills in both areas of expertise. We each learn about our unique skill sets through experience. Experience can come from both academic and real life situations. Consider your experience in your first five to 10 years of working. When you enter the work force you start out using the technical skills you learned from your education.

You then have to learn how to relate the close-ended problem solving skills from an academic environment to the open-ended problem solving skills required in the real world. In addition, your intelligence (IQ) and your personality (EQ) affect the way you develop and apply those open-ended problem solving skills. It is important to recognize this because, as I said, everyone is different and where they came from and where they are in their lives affect how people react to communication processes and styles.

As you moved through your journey to a leadership role, can you remember the first time being in a meeting with your boss, others at his/her level, and your boss's boss? You were the lowest level person in the room and you were invited because of the excellent work you did on the subject being discussed. You were excited to have been invited. You were proud of your work and anxious to show your ability in front of such a senior group! You were thinking about how you were going to contribute and perhaps even facilitate an outcome for success. When you were in the actual meeting you discovered that all the discussion was among the senior people and no one was asking your input or perspective. You tried to interject your brilliance only to realize that what you knew about the subject was only one small piece of the bigger picture. You may have felt less positive about your ability to contribute, or you could have become frustrated with the development process.

If you have experienced this example in your career, it is important to keep in mind how you felt and how you communicate/advise those that report to you when they have the opportunity to get this experience. The result on the development of the person in this example will depend on a number of subjective outcomes they feel about the experience. The point is that there is an opportunity, a teachable moment, where a subordinate can be coached by a more experienced mentor about the nature of the upcoming meeting and the learnings to be experienced.

You have a subordinate who shows potential. You understand from your own experiences that that associate needs experience to both encourage their confidence and help them learn how to use that confidence be effective in ways to leverage their abilities for success. You might mentor your subordinate by saying to them something like:

"Your first exposure to the group you are about to encounter includes many members above you in the organization, any of whom could have an impact on your career. The objective of the meeting is to decide some significant direction for the company. You should answer questions that are directed to you. There may not be any, but I will help if you get stuck on any subject. You don't have to volunteer to speak about the subject being discussed; rather I would suggest that you listen to the conversations, questions, and ideas that occur in the meeting. While you follow the questions being asked of the participants, think to yourself what you would recommend as an answer and compare those thoughts to the actual answers given by the people in the room. If you find that you are in line with the collective thinking of those who have more experience, your confidence should grow along with your experience. This will put you in a position to be more successful when it is your turn to participate."

What elements of respect do you see and feel in this example? Coaching, mentoring, encouragement, support, understanding, practice, training, experience sharing.

In addition to developing subordinates, the relationship with all areas of your business will help support your ability to lead and have people listen to you and be willing to learn new ways of doing things from you. To check on your relationship with associates you might ask yourself, "Do I know what people are doing in each of the critical process departments of my business?" I felt it was important for me to understand the business from their point of view in order to lead the changes necessary for the business to achieve desired results.

At each company I was with, I had a leadership role. I sought to understand the critical processes of the departments most remote from me. I was exposed to customer facing activities almost every day. On the other hand, manufacturing and sourcing departments were the most remote, and if I didn't make an attempt to connect with the associates in those departments, I would likely fail to develop the relationships necessary to lead. For each of the companies I led, I learned about issues with product flow, quality, safety, productivity, communication, and culture from the associates. I did this by working the first shift in each manufacturing department of the company. It was not some example of "Undercover Boss," rather it was a case of uncovered boss. I got to know people and people got to know me on a level of what we did and what we cared about. It is a foundation for respect. Some examples of my experience doing this are:

> Working on a glass fill line at a candle manufacturing company. In one operation the glass jars to be filled with wicks and wax were staged at the beginning of the fill line. The first operation on the line was to pick up a glass jar and glue a wick sustainer (a metal piece with a wick attached) to the bottom of the jar. The machine was indexed to take six jars across the line that corresponded with the filling nozzles

down the line. I don't remember what line speed the machine was set at, but I do know it was related to a standard cost we used to measure performance of the line. I quickly found out that I could not keep up with the requirement of getting six jars with wick sustainers glued in them at the front of the line in time for the machine to index forward. At times I felt the burn of the hot glue for the sustainer on my fingers and I was beginning to negatively affect the productivity of the line. The other workers on the front of the line were able to keep up with the machine and began to help me keep up as well. For many months after that the associates at the plant would joke with me that they had more recalls from the day I worked on the line. The relationships I developed from this experience allowed those associates and me to mutually challenge ourselves on how to get better and improve profitability in sustainable ways. Some of those ways did include automation!

➢ I worked on a liquid fill paint pen line for a well-known specialty chemical company. The line involved automatically indexing a pen body (three at a time) in a straight line while associates performed a number of in-line manual operations that involved gaskets and valve inserts before and after filling paint in those pens. It was eye opening how small the parts were for the manual assembly operations.

My fingers were literally too big to efficiently handle these parts with the speed and accuracy needed to keep up with the speed of the line. I also learned that the indexing of the line triggered vertigo in me, which led to feeling nauseous and/or faint at times while trying to perform the tasks. My performance became stuff of legends around there for quite some time. As in the example above, significant operational improvement was achieved at this company based on mutual respect; and this was a union plant.

➢ Another example involved a printing company where I worked in the press and bindery operations. I worked alongside the printing presses for a children's book line and gathered "signatures" (groups of pages printed on both sides of a single sheet that are folded and trimmed to create pages in a printed book). I learned the competitive advantage that our engineers had created over many years with respect to our ability to print and bind a particular type of book that we did for our largest customer. When I reviewed the profitability of those books, it was clear that we should have been able to reasonably charge more for those books than we did. The route to increased profitability was not in cost reduction in this case, rather, it was in charging the appropriate amount for a competitive advantage that was already created through our expertise in manufacturing. The result was a difficult but successful negotiation to increase our price to a more profitable level.

Regarding relationships, John Lanman, CEO Block and Co, summed it up nicely when he described the need for communication skill and the effect on relationships as:

"The biggest thing for me has been that I've learned that communication is key. Business is all about how well you communicate. It's not what you say, it's how you say it sometimes and that's a little extreme, but I do think building relationships and being approachable is really the key. I think as a leader its appeared to me that being approachable, being a regular guy, not being too separated, isolated, you know, relationship building, just getting out and talking to people and just building rapport has been probably the biggest thing. If you can't do that, if you don't have a connection, then nothing else you do is really going to matter because people ignore you. They don't identify with you. So being a successful leader really starts with being able to connect with people you're leading 1st and foremost."

Chapter 4

Connecting the Dots

Do you remember the picture puzzles that involved a series of dots and numbers? Some lines are already visible and then there are a series of numbers that you need to trace in numerical order. Some of these puzzles were more complicated and intricate than others. As you try to trace the numbers in the correct order you encounter some instances where the number patterns cross over others and you need to sort out the correct direction to connect the dots in the correct order. When you are successful, you get a clear picture of the subject and you can answer the question of what it is. Sound familiar? Does it also sound like trying to solve problems in your business?

As you know, business is like the picture puzzles I just referred to. In business there are many processes (puzzles) and steps within those processes (dots and numbers) that have to "connect" correctly and in the right sequence. There may even be some established connections (lines that already exist) that are easy to see and understand. Experience with a particular process can be very helpful in being able to complete the processes (puzzles) in a consistent manner to try and achieve the desired results. However, in business we commonly focus only on the connection of dots at the individual level within each process. I understand the logic of focusing on individual steps to get them correct and "repeatable." It would seem that if a process can be done correctly over and over again at the individual level, then each process will be done correctly and the business will succeed. The problem is at least two fold:

✓ The processes we are trying to complete is seldom as straight forward as following a sequential series of numbers already laid out on a page. The process steps required to achieve a desired result are affected by other factors that a business must anticipate but does not control.

✓ The focus on individual processes often leads to a lack of understanding and focus on connecting the dots across several key processes.

I worked for a major pharmaceutical company who was involved in manufacturing diagnostic test kits for a number of infectious diseases. The manufacturing process involved making components for the complete test kits separately. Each component was manufactured according to specific controlled processes, steps, and specifications that involved rigorous quality control checks and documented test results. To pass these tests meant that the component was successfully made according to the required specifications. The component was then stored and ready for inclusion in a "master" kit that included all of the components necessary to provide doctors and laboratories the ability to test patients for the possibility of having a significant, and in some cases, life threatening disease.

While it is critical for the components to be manufactured correctly according to specifications, it is also extremely important for each of the components to work together in the application of the overall test kit in order to provide a consistently accurate result. Fortunately, the pharmaceutical company did extend its rigorous control procedures to the maser kit level. There were a number of times internally when the individual components failed to work correctly in the master kit. These failures of course did not go to market; however, this example demonstrates how important it is to understand not just connecting the dots in individual processes, but knowing and connecting the dots across critical processes as well.

Business isn't always as complicated as chemistry. My experience informs me that while there are many processes with many steps that require attention to detail, the leadership of an organization can enhance the organization's ability to sustainably achieve exceptional results by understanding and managing the connections between the key mission and critical processes of the business. I have developed a graphic I call the ***World of Business.***

World of Business

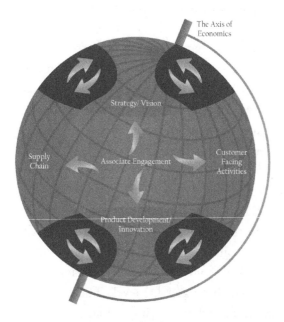

It can be a matter of opinion as to which challenges business leaders can and cannot control. Business intelligence tools and analytical techniques can significantly improve your ability to make decisions that result in more control of the challenges your business faces.

In business there are six critical process spheres that must be connected in order to optimize and sustain the sales and profits of an enterprise:

1. Strategy
2. Customer facing activities
3. Product development/innovation
4. Supply chain
5. Financial management
6. Associate engagement

Strategy is defined as a campaign on a broad scale to gain advantage over the competition. The strategy should leverage and allow for acquisition of the core competencies to gain competitive advantage. The strategy is the guiding plan that helps define priorities in each of the mission processes in the other five critical spheres of business process. The strategy must be aligned with the other five spheres and vice versa in order to optimize business results.

Customer facing activities define how your customers view your company, whether or not your company "qualifies" as a vendor, and if your company provides the "value" to the customer that gives you a sustainable competitive advantage over your competition. Customer facing activities involve any process that touches the customer. Included here are sales, marketing, service (orders on time and complete), logistics, product quality, and any other customer interaction.

Product development/innovation is ideally driven by requirements that come from outside the company as opposed to requirements internally. Strategy, customer facing activities, and research are sources for input into product development/innovation activities. Product development/innovation includes marketing, research, trend data, regulatory requirements, customer requirements, and quality.

Supply chain activities are essentially what they sound like. They are the chain of activities that allow the organization to supply a product (or services) to the customer. The product must be delivered in accordance with agreed upon product specifications, delivery times, quantities, locations, and logistics. Supply chain activities include manufacturing, finished product and component sourcing, inventory management, warehousing, and shipping. Information from customer facing activities, product development, and strategy is needed in order to optimize supply chain activities.

Financial management is essential to the accuracy of data transaction, aggregate records, and meeting the financing requirements of the business. Financial management includes cash flow management, internal controls, financial statement accuracy, and financing of the business. Without strong financial results, none of the other spheres of mission critical activities are possible.

Associate engagement may be the most important activity of all. It is critical that all associates understand the strategy of the business and the objectives of each of the mission critical processes embedded in the six spheres that they are involved in. Trust must be established with the associates in order to have them embrace the measurements required by the organization and candidly discuss action/corrective action plans necessary to continuously improve performance. This trust can lead to a culture of continuous improvement that drives the business to create sustainable profitable growth. Data must be made available to the appropriate associates in order for them to be able to make the best decisions possible.

Understanding the mission critical processes within these spheres is one key dimension of sustainable excellence in performance; the other key dimension is the connection between those mission critical processes. The connection between mission critical processes is like the electrical system in your home or office. It's the conduit of the energy that is available to make things work. This "conduit" gives your organization the ability to "turn the lights on and off," if you will. The "wiring" in that conduit that needs to be in place, maintained, and updated is your people and the technology that enables them.

Many organizations believe they have the processes they need to manage their business. The missing link to optimizing a business is the intelligence that connects those processes. While intelligence can be aided by technology, intelligence can only be executed by people. In other words, you can have all the processes and technology in place; however, if you don't have the right people, you cannot optimize the results of managing those processes. Your people will allow you to connect the six spheres the way they need to be in the business "world" that is your company and customers.

You can see in the diagram that the business world is indeed round, making it a continuum of connectivity that provides feedback to and from each of the six spheres of key business processes. The nucleus of this world is the people who interpret and communicate data and the axis around which this world rotates is financial management.

The use of respect and the concepts of recognizing and understanding how it affects you and those you deal with are key in engaging an organization across these six critical process spheres in business.

An example of this in practice is a global consumer products company where I was the COO for the North

American Wholesale Group. We designed, developed, manufactured, and sourced product globally. We marketed and distributed these consumer products to major retailers in the home décor segment in North America. In my experience one of the hardest business models to operate today is providing an in-line planogram of consumer products to major North American retailers with a lead time of up to 120 days. By the time the consumer standing in the aisle votes "no" you can have boats coming into Long Beach, California with product that won't sell. That product then becomes excess and/or obsolete inventory that you cannot recover you margins on, and in many cases, you will not even recover your cost. This is a significant problem that costs everyone in the supply chain (manufacturer, supplier, distributor, retailer, and ultimately the consumer) significant amounts of money and in many cases leads to business failure.

The solution to the problem was "connecting the dots." That may seem obvious; however, the critical related questions are:

- ➢ What dots? And…
- ➢ In what order of priority?

The problem for our company was that significant amounts of resources across supply chain, marketing, sales, management, and operations were spent on trying to design, make, and sell consumer products in our category that would fuel the growth and profitability of the business. In that sense our objective was the same as any for-profit business. We all know that time, human resources, and capital are in short supply when trying to execute our businesses. This shortage makes it critical that the processes that result in successful outcomes be done correctly and are designed to react to what the business controls and what it does not control. The missing link to success can be the connection between the critical processes.

When we looked at the major spheres of process, we began to break down the what, why, and how for the business in order to identify the connection points and order of priority. The following was intuitively known but not laid out in a way that would engage people to complete the task of connecting the right dots:

> Consumers wanted home décor products that they were emotionally connected to and were a sense of pride and self-fulfillment. The products needed to fit the consumers need state.

> Retailer's shelf space was like an Automatic Teller Machine (ATM) to them. In addition to having product that met consumer's needs, they needed to have product on the shelf when consumers were there to buy it.

> Given the logistics of receiving, storing, distributing, and filling shelves, there was a critical path of decision points that represented a lead time needed for the retailer to execute having product on the shelf.

> The product design processes of feature /functionality, innovation, value proposition, packaging, costs, pricing, and merchandising were elements of the critical path of decision points that represented a lead time needed for the supplier and working with the retailer to

have product ideas that could meet the needs of the consumer.

> The vetting of potential sources (including make vs buy) represented yet another series of lead times that needed to be managed and coordinated.

In the case of this consumer products company, the first "intra process" connection comes from the relationship with the customer. Helping the organization understand that across all the functions involved is a form of engagement that starts with respect. A former executive colleague of mine, Steve Kosmalski, gave me some advice based on his experience that taught me how to approach the complex puzzle of leading the varied groups of people through this type of process. He had significant experience in sales and marketing. Using a marketing brand development meeting as an example he explained:

> *"I could get everyone in a room and begin to tell them what to consider, how to look at the situation, and how to proceed with brand and product development step by step in about half an hour…or I could explain the objective and it could take them four hours to work it out as I facilitate their learning. My counsel, always take the four hours. That way, they will internalize the process and own it."*

Steve believed engaging associates with the following principles:

> ➢ Inclusion of staff into decision making processes and key initiative identification

> ➢ Communication across the enterprise

> ➢ Passing on whatever I learned to those I work with when appropriate - coaching

> ➢ Recognizing and honoring key non-work elements in associates lives

> ➢ Humor - as much as possible

Engaging your people and having them understand and feel how what they do impacts the bigger picture is a form of respect that builds confidence. If you want people to be assertive, even appropriately aggressive, they need to have confidence. Even with our children we want them to be successful, yet how do we go about trying to get them to be assertive/aggressive? After decades of coaching youth sports (soccer, basketball, baseball) I have witnessed a number of situations. The one that is almost universal is that parents want their child to be the one who scores the goal or makes a tremendous play defending the goal. We love our children and care deeply for them, yet in order to "encourage" our children to be assertive/aggressive we shout at them from the stands. We shout commands of what to do and how to do it.

The reality is that kids will be as assertive as they can be when they are most confident. People don't feel confident unless they can learn and master skill on their own time table. Certainly there is no harm in exposing them to pressure, but the type and timing of pressure can make a huge difference between a person who embraces the challenge and a person who is just going through the motions. The latter will not be able to sustain or accelerate performance.

I find this holds true for adults as well as children. Since leadership is ultimately tasked with achieving results, it is important to recognize what the timetable for learning and mastering is for each person. We all know that people in our organizations are not always the right fit for a particular position they may be in, and in those cases a change needs to be made. You may not realize that everyone is "watching" before, during, or after the change is made. It is important to you and your organization that the change process be handled with respect and not the result of someone has stopped trying to doing their job because they can't take the pressure of being shouted at about what/how they should do their job.

With the wise counsel of a colleague and the ability to remember what brings out the most positive assertiveness in people, confidence, we began to tackle the task of connecting the critical "dots." Product development and innovation are a critical starting point. It is best left to the experts like my colleague. Perhaps you have that background and tackle it yourself; however, I would recommend that the CEO's job is to facilitate across functions/processes and not so much within functions/processes. If you hire the right people with the right skills to handle the functions and processes you won't run the risk of getting sucked in too deep in an organization and not effectively leading the entire organization.

The next concurrent connecting of processes is to

connect your product development process with your customer's product introduction process. How we began to do this was to engage associates who had roles that touched our product development process. This included all the associates that touched our customer's product introduction process and anyone in between. Those people cut across the following functions in our organization:

Sales – owns the relationship with the buyer and should know:

> ➢ The customer's timetable for product introductions
> ➢ Market trends
> ➢ Product feature/functionality requirements
> ➢ Product lead times

Sourcing – owns the relationship with procurement partners (manufacturing & suppliers) and should know:

> ➢ Market/customer trends
> ➢ The customer's timetable for product introductions
> ➢ Product lead times
> ➢ Product feature/functionality
> ➢ Product specifications
> ➢ Product development/innovation pipeline

Marketing – owns product development/innovation and should know:

> ➢ Market/customer trends

> ➤ The customer's timetable for product introductions
> ➤ Product feature/functionality
> ➤ Product specifications
> ➤ Product lead times

Manufacturing – owns supply processes owned or contracted and should know:

> ➤ The customer's timetable for product introductions
> ➤ Product feature/functionality
> ➤ Product specifications
> ➤ Market trends
> ➤ Product lead times
> ➤ Product development/innovation pipeline

Warehousing – owns storage and handling of products and materials and should know:

> ➤ The customer's timetable for product introductions
> ➤ Lead times
> ➤ Product specifications

Distribution – owns product logistics and should know:

> ➤ The customer's timetable for product introductions
> ➤ Lead times
> ➤ Product specifications

Quality – owns compliance and should know:

> ➤ Product feature/functionality
> ➤ Product specifications

Looking at these responsibilities and relationships in a graphic format highlights the three key functions of marketing, sourcing, and manufacturing. The chart demonstrates that these three functions are critical players in the coordinated execution of "spheres" of critical processes that drive the performance of a business. When businesses operate more in functional silos, those businesses miss the proactive collaboration needed. In my experience, those businesses have significantly underperformed their potential and in some cases have gone out of business.

Connecting the Dots: Table of Process Knowledge Sharing						
Function / Key Processes	Customer Timetable	Market/ Customer Trends	Product Feature/ Functionality	Product Development /Innovation	Product Lead Times	Product Specifications
Sales	X	X	X		X	
Marketing	X	X	X	X	X	X
Quality			X			X
Sourcing	X	X	X	X	X	X
Manufacturing	X	X	X	X	X	X
Distribution	X				X	X
Warehousing	X				X	X

Helping the people in your organization understand the critical relationships across and between these functions is important on a number of levels. From a process standpoint it may seem obvious. From an associate development and cultural development standpoint it may even be more important. How many of you have experienced the ups and downs in the performance of your business due to the changes in understanding and collaboration across these functions?

Consider the following situation I encountered in business. The company is in the consumer product segment. See if you recognize some of the challenges described here from an actual company.

North American retailers and being challenged from all angles! The online explosion of organizations offering product for sale in every category is unending. Trying to figure out the buying habits and trends of very different generations requires expensive research with questionable insights. The right mix of brand equity versus private label value expectations is a constantly moving target. Trying to maintain margins in an environment of significant competition for the same or similar product in the same categories in the face of the fixed infrastructure of outlets and distribution is very challenging. In addition, the logistics of long lead time sourcing channels makes competing at retail in North America very stressful and many times an emotional roller coaster.

These issues and challenges are magnified for suppliers to the North American retail channel, as retailers put enormous pressure on their suppliers because of the pressures they face. To solve this problem I started with the need for connections between functions and processes as shown in the chart above. I then began discussing those connections with leadership in those functions. By engaging those folks and demonstrating the value I placed on their help in solving this complicated business problem, they brought the best thinking of the organization to bear. The issues identified from the collective brain power of the organization were:

> The timetable for our retail customers from product review to putting product on shelf was 18 months.

> The lead time for product development from research to quotes from prospective suppliers (both internal and external) was six months.

> The lead time for offshore supply chain was four months.

> Some of these steps can be accomplished concurrently, but most need to be done consecutively. The total lead time from product concept to placement of shelf is at least 30 months (2.5 years).

> If the process is performed out of sequence:

- Sales will decline
- Margins will likely decline
- Your resources will be inefficient at best and leave your company at its worst
- The impact of non-sellable inventory (excess and obsolete) can be significant

> There is a significant difference in the effect of lead times on new product load-ins versus replenishment of product that sells and replacement of product that doesn't sell.

While this information was available and in fact known in several areas of the organization, it was not shared across the organization. When I say not shared, I am referring to sharing information with the understanding that the process for being successful involves designing a cross functional process with collaboration on managing the steps in that process. When people are involved in the understanding of the connection of their functional areas and the identification of the critical elements that affect their processes, they learn how to be better at their jobs and they make a better contribution to creating sustainable profitable growth.

The result of the engagement of associates in learning how what they are doing is related to the overall objectives of performance of the organization will be significant and sustainable. In the case I described, we developed the following solutions:

> ➤ Aligned and integrated key processes/functions to optimize strategy execution in a sustainable way.
> ➤ Energized associates about their roles and contributions to the organization.
> ➤ Recognized the "hidden" costs of product execution, most notably freight and non-sellable inventory.
> ➤ Developed and implemented a hybrid manufacturing/sourcing strategy that involved shorter lead time solutions for replenishment versus initial placement.

Chapter 5

Understanding Results

As I previously mentioned, my belief is that leadership is an equal emphasis on results and relationships. From my experience, the secrets of leadership that are discussed in many of the chapters relate to the relationship side of this equation. The ability to build relationships is certainly the "missing link" in how to lead effectively. That ability; however, needs to go hand in hand with the ability to understand and focus on actual and expected results. In this context, expected results should define success for your organization. As you know, focusing on the wrong expected or actual results will be detrimental to your organization. If you want to empower your associates to work independently to create sustainable profitable growth, you need to lead them with the right metrics, visibility, and access to the right data to make decisions.

Many companies focus first and foremost on revenue growth. This makes sense because revenue growth can provide the cash needed to pay bills and investment in the business. There are times when a major focus on revenue growth should go hand in hand with other significant metrics that relate to the success of that revenue growth in providing cash to the company. One example is a company that I was asked to lead. When I got there the company had experienced significant revenue declines for a number of years that resulted in putting the company in a seriously bad financial condition. When assessing the strategy I asked the leadership team for their thoughts on what the company should do to turn things around. One of the first answers I was told was that there should be a focus on revenue and that we needed to hire a sales person who had "grazing rights" at Walmart to get our products back on shelf there. I replied, "While I completely understand why this was suggested, I have one key question." When asked what my question was I asked, "What is our service level?" People looked at me and said they didn't know what their service level was and did not even know how to calculate it. I told them that service level is a measure of shipments that are complete and on time. We calculated our service level and discovered that it was 47%!

If we had hired someone with a reputation that could get us back on shelf at Walmart, or any other major retailer, we would have lost the business again in a short period of time. Until we recognized and took steps to fix the service level we would not have been successful growing revenue with those retailers, and we would have damaged our ability to ever grow sales successfully in that critical channel for us.

At other companies where I held a leadership role we

inherited issues with lack of visibility to the return on customer investments and how they should be managed, not only to grow sales, but also to grow profitability. The examples in this chapter that follow are how I helped people in my organization understand the relationship of spending to revenue growth and profitability.

One of the issues I have seen time and time again in my career is that the metrics used to provide feedback to associates and their company on how they are doing are traditional financial statements and/or "key performance indicators" (KPI's). In many cases it is difficult at best to relate those KPI's to financial results and vice versa.

Financial statements are widely used as the "report card" for business. Financial statements follow rules of accounting and are supposed to communicate a description of results in categories that drive a business to the reader. The income statement is a lens for analyzing the earnings of a business. This chapter will examine the income statement in accounting terms and how it falls short of providing critical analytical information to make decisions. You will be introduced to a more detailed analytical approach for understanding the profitability drivers of your business that I call the **Direct Variable Profitability (DVP) model**. I have used this model in a number of businesses with exceptional results in visibility and clarification of drivers of profitability leading to sustainable profitable growth. The data in this example is not the actual data from one of the companies I referred to due to confidentiality. The issues and analytical techniques are real. The example company information illustrates data elements to consider when analyzing drivers of profitability and to compare that visibility to what you see in the traditional accounting income statements.

The DVP Model will allow you to better understand the drivers of profitability of your business and prioritize resources to manage those drivers. This approach can be used in any business for any reporting period. Use of the DVP model is restricted only by the tools that you have available to access data in your systems.

The Profit and Loss Statement

Table 1
Example company P&L statement (in thousands)

	Year 1	Year 2
Sales	$10,000	$12,000
Cost of Sales	$6,000	$7,200
Gross Profit	$4,000	$4,800
Percentage of Sales	40.0%	40.0%
Selling Expenses	$2,000	$2,500
Percentage of Sales	20.0%	20.8%
General and Administrative expenses	$1,000	$1,200
Percentage of Sales	10.0%	10.0%
Net Income/(Loss)	$1,000	$1,100
Percentage of Sales	10.0%	9.2%

It's likely that you have seen what is commonly called a profit and loss statement (P&L) or an income statement. A P&L statement defines profit as being equal to revenue (sales), less all costs and expenses. Seems fairly straightforward; however, it is rarely obvious what action to take just by looking at this financial statement. Consider a company that has the P&L statement shown in Table 1.

Based on this statement, can you tell how the company is

doing? And what it should do differently going forward? On the surface, the company seems to have grown sales by 20%, gross profit by 20%, and improved the profits by 10%. Seems like a winning accomplishment. But what does it really mean? For example, a company might grow its sales and profits in the first quarter of year two over the previous year and think they are successful. However, it could be that the company is unaware of or does not have visibility into a number of factors that influenced the sales dollars—factors that indicate a problem. Many factors affecting profitability (i.e., the relationship of expenses to sales) are critical to understanding your business and its potential. Those relationships can be defined by the following categories of cost and expenses:

➢ **Variable costs**—costs that vary directly with unit movement. Examples are material costs, volume discounts, labor to make the product, and so on.

➢ **Fixed costs**—costs that do not vary directly with unit movement. Examples are the cost of your office building, management salaries, security, insurance, and so on.

➢ **Step variable costs**—costs that are fixed in the short term and more variable over the mid-term. You should not get too hung up on these types of costs. It is better to make some simplifying assumptions. If costs seem relatively fixed in the short term, then classify them as fixed for analysis purposes.

It is important for you and your associates to know how your costs behave relative to the product (unit) movement of your business. The behavior here refers to whether the costs are variable (they go up when unit movement goes up and go down when unit movement goes down) or fixed (do not move directly with unit movement). This is essentially a contribution margin approach. To illustrate, Table 2 shows the example P&L from earlier in the chapter and breaks out some of the underlying data.

Table 2
Example Company P&L statement (in thousands)

	Year 1	Year 2	Percent Change	Type (1)
Gross Sales	$11,000	$13,200		Variable
Customer Returns & Allowances (2)	$1,000	$1,200		Variable
Net Sales	$10,000	$12,000	20.0%	
Direct Material	$3,000	$3,600	20.0%	Variable
Direct Labor	$500	$600	20.0%	Variable
Depreciation	$1,000	$1,000	0%	Fixed
Supervision	$1,500	$1,500	0%	Fixed
Other Manufacturing	$0	$500	N/A	????
Total Cost of Sales	$6,000	$7,200	20.0%	
Gross Profit	$4,000	$4,800		
Percentage of Sales	40.0%	40.0%		
Co-op Advertising	$300	$760	153.3%	Variable
Commissions	$200	$240	20.0%	Variable
Salaries	$1,500	$1,500	0%	Fixed
Total Selling Expenses	$2,000	$2,500	25.0%	
Percentage of Sales	20.0%	20.8%		
General & Administrative Expenses	$1,000	$1,200	20.0%	Fixed
Percentage of Sales	10.0%	10.0%		
Net Income/(Loss)	$1,000	$1,100	10.0%	
Percentage of Sales	10.0%	9.2%		

Type means how the values behave with respect to unit volume. Customer programs can include returns and allowances for volume, merchandising, seasonal promotions, defectives, shortages, and return to stock.

When you look at the same P&L with a classification of how costs behave, you begin to see a clearer picture of the business. The result is that there is potentially more actionable information that requires further analysis. In this case:

> If the classification of fixed and variable costs within the total cost of sales is correct, there is an unexplained increase in cost of sales of $500K This could be driven by a number of issues that need to be addressed, such as:

  - Did material prices rise significantly?
  - Did material utilization get worse?
  - Did labor productivity get worse?
  - Did salaries in fixed overhead increase too much compared to the manufacturing activity?

> In selling expenses, why did co-op advertising increase at a rate of 7.5 times the sales increase?

> In general expenses, why did fixed general and administrative expenses increase the same rate as sales?

You get the picture. The existence of these questions does not mean the business is mismanaged. They should not be "gotcha" types of questions about the business. They are fundamental questions necessary to understand the business. The answers to these questions lead toward the right actions to take.

The Direct Variable Profitability (DVP) Model

When you define these classifications of fixed and variable expenses in terms of your business, you can begin to analyze your business more in depth. We call this in-depth analytical technique the *direct variable profitability model (DVP)*. There are three steps to creating this model:

1. Classify revenues and costs as variable or fixed status as they relate to unit movement. This will replace the standard classification based on functional P&L lines without regard to how they behave.

2. Group revenues and costs in categories that are directly accountable for them. The activities in these categories directly drive the costs. These categories are called **direct categories of accountability (DCAs)**. They are:

➢ **Product**—includes prices, allowances, deductions, costs, and volume at the unit level that are directly related to the product itself. The profitability measured here can be for a single product or group of products.
➢ **Customer**—includes prices, allowances, deductions, costs, volume, and programs for all units directly related to the customer itself. The profitability measured here can be for a single customer or a group of customers.
➢ **Channel**—includes a roll-up of variable and fixed revenue/ costs directly related to all customers in a given channel of distribution.
➢ **Region**—includes a roll-up of information for all customers in a given region.
➢ **Department**—includes all costs that relate to expense

line items that are in a department or group of departments and are not directly related to unit volume. Some of these department expenses are directly related to a region, channel, or customer, and some are related to the overall period being measured. The activities that cause spending in this DCA will vary depending on expense type.

3. Arrange the information in the P&L starting with data which are directly related to unit movement (variable) at the top and add data which are not directly related to unit movement (fixed) below the variable data until you have completely rearranged the statement. It is important to note that the Net Income line should be the same total as it was before this exercise. The sample P&L from earlier in this chapter would now look like Table 3 on the next page.

The analysis now reveals issues that were not visible in the original P&L and were still not obvious in the second version. The questions about the business that are important to understand are:

> Variable margins are declining and are driven by co-op advertising expenses rising faster than sales. Is the business getting the return they should out of their investment in co-op advertising?

> Why don't we see the impact of productivity and cost reduction programs in the variable costs?

➤ What is the nature of the "other manufacturing" costs and what is driving it?

➤ Again, why are fixed general and administrative expenses going up at the same rate as sales?

Table 3
Example Company P&L statement using the DVP Model
(in thousands)

	Year 1	Year 2	Percent Change	Type (1)
Gross Sales	$11,000	$13,200	20.0%	Variable
Customer Returns & Allowances (2)	$1,000	$1,200	20.0%	Variable
Net Sales	$10,000	$12,000	20.0%	
Co-op Advertising	$300	$760	153.3%	Variable
Direct Material	$3,000	$3,600	20.0%	Variable
Direct Labor	$500	$600	20.0%	Variable
Commissions	$200	$240	20.0%	Variable
Total Direct Cost of Sales	$4,000	$5,200	30.0%	
Direct Contribution Margin	$6,000	$6,800	13.3%	
Percentage of Sales	60.0%	56.7%		
Depreciation	$1,000	$1,000	0%	Fixed
Supervision	$1,500	$1,500	0%	Fixed
Other Manufacturing	$0	$500	N/A	???
Sales & Marketing Salaries	$1,500	$1,500	0%	Fixed
General & Administrative Expenses	$1,000	$1,200	20.0%	Fixed
Total Fixed Costs	$5,000	$5,700	14.0%	
Percentage of Sales	50.0%	47.5%		
Net Income/(Loss)	$1,000	$1,100	10.0%	
Percentage of Sales	10.0%	9.2%		

(1) Type means how the values behave with respect to unit volume.
(2) Customer programs can include returns and allowances for volume, merchandising, seasonal promotions, defectives, shortages, and return to stock.

Each line in the P&L should be linked to someone in your organization who has direct responsibility for the activities that drive those results as well as the actual results. The analysis process should continue as a "deep dive" into a line item that is significantly different than expectations. The ability to build the model and do the deep dive analysis where necessary will likely require locating and extracting data from your system very differently than you do today.

Deep Dive Example

Sales are areas in which companies definitely benefit from a deep dive analysis! The analysis of sales beyond aggregate sales performance can reveal actionable issues about your business that are not visible at an aggregate level. Some of the key drivers for sales are price and mix. These drivers had little or no visibility in the traditional analytical reporting of sales results. The same benefit comes from a deep dive into other areas of the P&L. The exhibits in this chapter demonstrate that the DVP model of a P&L helps to identify less visible areas that need further understanding and action.

Through the example in this chapter we revealed that there are costs that behave differently than expected and have had a negative impact on earnings. One example of this is co-op advertising. Co-op advertising is an investment in advertising with your customer (the customer typically places the ad) aimed at driving sales growth. It should be an expense that is directly variable with sales. In other words, as advertising investment increases, your sales should increase. In the example, the fact that this expense and sales did not behave this way should be a cause for concern:

- ➤ Was the timing of the investment correctly made
- ➤ Was the money actually used to place the advertising by the customer?
- ➤ Were the ads properly designed to drive the sales of the intended product(s)?
- ➤ Was a volume increase in fact offset by other pricing actions within the sales line?

This last question can lead to going into more detail on other "investments" in your customers to understand why sales may not have increased more than reported. You might be aware of some of the "investments" in customers to drive your sales. Many of these customer investments are really forms of price adjustments and may not be providing a return to the company making the investment. Some examples other than co-op advertising are:

- ➤ Payment term discounts
- ➤ Volume discounts back to dollar one each year
- ➤ Off-invoice discounts (such as freight, merchandising, and seasonal promotion allowances)
- ➤ Foregoing price increases

The effect that these customer investments can have on your business is hidden in a comparison to aggregate lagging indicators. Sales dollars may not be growing as much as expected, but unless you can analyze these investments you may not know why and what it means in terms of how your customers view the real value of your product. Another area of the example P&L that is shown to require a deeper analysis is the "fixed" departmental spending. Looking at fixed and variable department expenses separately allows you to:

> Identify areas of concern sooner than if they are allocated. When costs are combined (allocated) they tend to lose their identity. It gets further complicated if we combine (allocate) costs that behave differently from one another. For example, costs that are fixed combined with variable cost will make it difficult to understand what is driving those costs—volume activity or a completely different set of activities.
> Identify activities that drive spending more accurately.
> Identify who in your organization is accountable and responsible for these activities and spending decisions more directly.
> Identify when no one has been given the accountability and responsibility for the activities and spending in any area.

Measurements are critical to the management process. As leaders we must be able to both understand and explain measurements to each of our constituents where appropriate:

> Associates
> Customers
> Shareholders
> Suppliers
> Investors

Chapter 6

SEE the HOW

Most of us have either seen golf or played golf. Very few of us have mastered the golf swing to the point of sustainable success. Hitting a golf ball seems like it should be straightforward enough. After all, it is one of the only sports involving hitting a ball when the ball is not moving. Simple! You just walk up to a stationary ball sitting on the ground and hit it with a club. That's it, right?

I'm not an expert when it comes to golf; however, I have been known to occasionally impersonate a golfer. We have been told that there are a number of components to the golf swing:

- ✓ Grip
- ✓ Posture
- ✓ Stance

✓ Shoulder turn (back swing)
✓ Tempo
✓ Swing "on plane" (down swing)

There are probably more components from a technical perspective, but these are the ones I can recognize as the minimum components that have an effect on the result of the shot. Before we begin to execute these processes, we are told to stand behind the ball, look at the view in front of us, identify a target that fits with the situation in front of us, visualize the shot, then execute the components of the swing noted above without thinking about them by employing a concept called "muscle memory." Are you starting to get tense just thinking about it? We are supposed to be able to execute the components of the golf swing without thinking about it, but it is more difficult to master muscle memory in golf than it seems from the outside looking in. Personally, I do more thinking in my backswing than I did all during college!

Having sustainable success in the game of golf, like many other sports, can be a metaphor for sustainable success in business. Consider the following components of business success:

➤ Understanding the markets and customers for your business (standing behind the ball to look at the view in front of you)
➤ Setting a mission (identifying a target that allows you to be successful in shooting the lowest score)
➤ Creating a strategy (visualizing the shot that will help produce the lowest score)
➤ Executing key processes that should be aligned with

the strategy, also known as connecting the dots (executing the components of the golf swing)

➢ Getting the feedback from execution and making adjustments as needed (finding the ball and addressing the next shot with updated input about the situation and target)

These activities that I have described are known in academic terms as "The Management Process." It is not a new concept; in fact, it has been around for centuries. The struggle has been how to develop an organization that can connect all of these activities (dots) in a way that is aligned properly and is repeatable in a sustainable way. Traditionally, the solution implemented to do this is an organizational structure of functional responsibilities (sales, operations, finance, etc.) and a hierarchy of "leadership" (President, Vice President, Director, Manager, etc.). As you think of this structure as it exists at your business, what comes to mind when you think of barriers to results? We should leave the personal style dislikes aside, at least for now... remember we should all try to respect each other first...

The structure of functional responsibilities and hierarchy of leadership that exist in most businesses today are certainly what I have experienced. When I think about the barriers that existed and, in some cases were perpetuated, the word that comes to mind is silos. The silos created by the typical business structure and the behavior that they instill, reinforce, and perpetuate can lead to some of the most significant barriers to success in business.

The World of Business™ graphic in this book depicts the challenge of the interrelationship of the critical spheres of the business process. Connecting those spheres while using the concept of the Management Process may seem like an impossible task at times. Many people with varied experience have tried to describe systematic, process driven solutions to solve this puzzle.

So what ties all of these elements and levels together?

There is a common thread throughout these sometimes complicated required connections....**people**. By definition, people are complicated and can be unpredictable. They are most unpredictable when they are force fit into a process that they are not suited for, don't understand how their role makes a difference, or are not engaged to participate in the objectives. The first circumstance of people force fit in a process they are not suited for is an issue of the skills needed. That issue alone could, and has, filled libraries with books on how to address it. We will not cover that here.

The last two circumstances of people not understanding their role, or not being engaged to participate, are issues of leadership and respect. In my experience, there is no written formula as to when and how to respect people in every situation you may encounter. Gaining an awareness of the Emotional Scale that I describe in this book, and where you are on that scale at key moments is a critical skill. Learning your triggers that move you up or down the scale will be an equally critical skill for maximizing you success when dealing with others.

The puzzle of the World of Business is understandably complicated to solve. In an attempt to create an innovative solution, many learned folks have tried to simplify the points of connection involved and the focus points required to solve the puzzle. Many consultants and business leaders have expressed the view that setting the correct strategy, the

WHAT, for the business is most important. Others have stated that understanding the emotional engagement of associates and customers, the **WHY**, is most important. Still others say that focus on execution, the **HOW**, is the most critical. Each of these areas of focus is indeed critical. So why do so many businesses fail to create sustainable profitable growth?

I believe the point that is missing in these debates is the practical connection between all three areas that require focus and how they overlay the environment in which they exist. The golf swing on a golf course is a perfect example of what I mean. The environment can change with each shot, which can dictate the use and technique of the components of the golf swing; however, the mission of shooting the lowest score possible remains the same. So the puzzle needs to be solved by utilizing all three elements of **WHAT**, **WHY**, and **HOW**.

When I have been successful in solving the puzzle, I have looked at its **S**trategy, **E**ngagement, and **E**xecution (which spell the word **SEE)** and noticed that **HOW** encompasses the interrelationship of all three. In other words, **SEE the HOW.** Answering the **HOW** correctly means answering the **WHAT** and **WHY** correctly. In addition, I have learned over time, a number of times the hard way, that engagement and execution involve respect. Respect involves getting people to believe in themselves and that IF you succeed in getting people to believe in themselves, they will set bigger goals on their own.

Leadership involves bringing people together. The management process should be one where an objective is identified that would result in success for all those involved if achieved. Notice that I said success for all. That does not imply that success is the same for each person. Success should be as closely tied to the contribution of each individual involved in achieving the desired successful result as possible. The equity of the evaluation of the contribution does have a subjective component, and by definition not everyone will agree with the evaluation. Leadership does not focus on the fairness of a situation. Focusing on the fairness in most situations will trigger a negative response on the Emotional Scale. True Leadership will focus on the situation with respect and therefore solution options instead of disappointment and possible blame.

Back to the leadership role—it involves an equal emphasis on results and relationships. It is 100/100 not 50/50. Many people believe that this reference to relationships relates to the relationship of the leader to his/her associates.

That is partly true. In fact the leadership emphasis regarding relationships relates to all relationships.

The idea of controlling emotions is critical to successful leadership. This concept is different from the mere requirement of achieving results. There have been numerous examples in business where results, even significant results, were achieved even when the emotions of those in charge were damaging to relationships. Those results are rarely sustainable. Leaders who control their emotions in the face of crisis or challenges and actually respect and serve others are successful in creating *sustainable* results.

I know the pressures and stress of conflict are a lot to deal with. These pressures and stress can rise exponentially in the face of uncertain success when trying as hard as you can. You may feel that your situation is more stressful than what others are going through. Let me ask you, where would you rank being in a war zone compared to your work situation?

I think that most of us can agree that even our worst perceived work environment would take a back seat to a combat zone during war. Members of each of our armed services can be put in harm's way and faced with actual life or death situations when involved in a war. With that in mind, consider this: Every major service of the U.S. Armed Forces uses the word and concept of RESPECT which is written into their core values.

MARINE CORPS VALUES: *"To respect human dignity; and to have respect and concern for each other"*

ARMY VALUES: *"Respect. Rely upon the golden rule. How we consider others reflects upon each of us, both personally and as a professional organization."*

NAVY VALUES: *"Accordingly, we will: Demand respect up and down the chain of command; Care for the safety, professional, personal, and spiritual well-being of our people; Show respect toward all people without regard to race, religion, or gender; Treat each individual with human dignity; Be committed to positive change and constant improvement."*

AIR FORCE VALUES: *"Respect for others. Service before self tells us also that a good leader places the troops ahead of his/her personal comfort. We must always act in the certain knowledge that all persons possess fundamental worth as human beings."*

In addition there was a recent U.S. Army radio commercial titled, "Respect: *Before you can earn respect you have to earn your place on this team.*"

Speaking of war, there are many lessons from the strategy and tactics of battles in history. There are also lessons on organizational structure and leadership style regarding communication and respect. While there are a number of examples of famous battles involving these lessons (e.g. Custer's last stand), one famous battle in history that demonstrates the effect on results of organizational behavior is the battle of Gettysburg. While attending training at the U.S. Army War College in Carlisle Pennsylvania I had the fortune of attending lectures from instructors on the dynamics of the leadership that significantly affected the battle of Gettysburg and its outcome. Supporting the in-classroom training were in-field sessions of actually walking the battlefields of nearby Gettysburg.

The Confederate Army was led by the famous Robert E. Lee. Lee was beloved by nearly all who served in the Army of Northern Virginia (the primary military force of the Confederate Army). It seems that an organization having its members believe in their leader would be a positive thing. Too much of a good thing can be counterproductive to your goals in any number of endeavors; however, and in this case it was a problem exacerbated by the fact that Robert E. Lee did not delegate that same respect to many other leaders in his organization, nor could he be accessible to everyone in order to communicate the message of what he wanted directly to the people in his organization. He did, in fact, have one person in a leadership role who he trusted enough to delegate to: General Stonewall Jackson.

The problem was that General Jackson was killed in the

battle of Chancellorsville, Virginia a few months before the battle of Gettysburg. Without his "right hand man," General Lee initially put Jackson's army in the hands of General Ewell and then to General Early. Neither of these officers was as experienced or skilled in battlefield techniques and neither had the relationship and trust with General Lee. Lee spent little to no time communicating with either of them to help them learn/understand what he wanted. The result was that the leadership on the battlefield didn't know what to do in the battle of Gettysburg and the rank and file was looking for word directly from Lee, who had his hands full with other matters at the battle. This issue cost the Confederate Army the ability to take Cemetery Hill, and military experts believe ultimately led to the loss at Gettysburg.

The organizational structure of the leader at the top being the only beacon for direction and the failure of that leader to communicate with and train his subordinates led to the loss of a critical objective in the battle and ultimate loss of the war to competition.

On the other side, the Army of the Potomac (the Union Army), operated with a more delegated authority structure, and included battlefield commanders that had the experience and autonomy to manage the battle according to what was happening on the front lines. Their ability to react more quickly and with better instincts honed through actual training and experience and with the trust of the senior ranks created a competitive advantage that allowed them to win in the face of situation that could have easily been a loss.

How you are structured and communicate makes a big difference. General Douglas McArthur is quoted as saying,

"Never give an order that can't be obeyed;" while in the words of Sophocles, "What you cannot enforce, do not command." Leslie Pockell author of the book *The 100 Greatest Leadership principles of all time,* points out that they both appear to be saying the same thing, but not quite. She goes on to say that "Sophocles focusses on the leader, and McArthur focuses on the led;" thus, the multidimensional requirement of leadership is, in my opinion, embodied in respect. The risk regarding relationships in pursuit of successful results is in focusing exclusively on results.

I interviewed Elliott Greenberg who is the owner and CEO of JC Licht, a company in the retail paint and decorating space. His story about a high potential associate achieving great success through the application of communication in demonstrating respect is a great example of helping someone see the HOW to be a more effective as a leader. Elliott recounted the following story:

> *"I have an employee now, one of my district managers, who is one of the hardest working people I've ever seen in my life. He's just very task driven. I just felt that he was rushing through the relationship part of the job. We were growing a lot, opening a lot of stores. He has too many stores. I need to hire a 3rd district manager, but he's so wanting to get everything done himself.*
>
> *He'd go in the store, "everybody good?" Do what he had to do and run to the next store. I got the sense in talking to my people that he wasn't listening to them. One day, I texted him over the weekend and I said, "Could you come in the office Monday morning?" and I just had a heart to heart*

with him. I told him how great he is, how much I respect how hard he works, how he's so bright. He's a great person. I'm so happy he's a district manager and I said, "but one of the things I think I created for you is I'm putting a lot of stress on you......I want you to take a step back." He goes, "What do you mean?" I go, "I want you to spend more time talking to our people. I want you to spend time hugging them and thanking them. I know that's how you feel, because you fight for them for raises and you speak so highly of our people, but sometimes you don't take the time to let them know."

It wasn't because he didn't believe it. He would say I'm too busy, too busy. I said slow down. I asked him. I said," Have I ever told you that you didn't get something done? We talk every day on the phone and we meet at least once a week. Did I ever question why you didn't get something done?" He goes, "No you haven't." I go, "You're creating that stress for yourself. The most important thing to me is that you're a leader, you're a district manager. You have 17 stores. You probably have 125 employees that you see and talk to on a weekly, biweekly basis."

Make everyone feel special. Talk. Get to know them all. Let them know how much we appreciate them. Get insights from them on what we're doing right and what we're doing wrong. I find more about my company from the lowest person on the totem pole than I do from the manager, always. I go and I'll have a conversation with them.

We had an event in Dallas Grove, so I stopped

there to say hi to everyone. I will take each employee, wait until they're done with their customers and say, 'You have a minute?" Then I talk and say, "How are we doing? How are you doing? Do you like the job? What's the most challenging? Are you getting along with everyone? What's your long term goal?"

I'm not giving you all the questions, but at least two or three I ask every time. They just talk. They open up and they trust me. They love that I talk to them --The owner's talking to me. We have a lot of new people. They can't believe the owner comes here and he talks to us. I never want to lose that, but I don't want just the owner to do that. I want all my leadership to do that....not just me doing it.

Sometime, after having this discussion with my District Manager, I spent a little time in Dallas Grove. One of our other senior management is a woman we hired there. She's been with us only about six months, but she's dynamic. She and her team had a meeting with the District Manager I talked to yesterday. I saw her later in the office in the day and I said, "How'd the meeting go?" She replied, "It was a very important meeting. There were some issues that we had to address. I don't know what kind of drug he was on, but he was unbelievable. I didn't have to do anything. He...was just so warm. He helped them understand the issues. He must have had like, a lobotomy over the weekend."

I had that talk with my District Manager, he got it right away, and he didn't question it He *goes, "You're 100 percent right. I'm so thankful that you told me that my actions could be so much more respectful." I know he's a good person and he is not disrespectful."*

This story illustrates the benefit of being respectful to our associates even about constructive criticism, and in turn having our associates employ respect to help teams work effectively and proactively on solving issues.

A famous Greek historian Polybius said, "Those who know how to win are more numerous than those who know how to make proper use of their victories." Relatedly, Leo Tolstoy, regarded as one of the greatest authors of all time once wrote, "Many people have ideas on how others should change; few people have ideas on how they should change." The lesson from these great thinkers and leaders is that we should never stop learning about who we are and how we act/react in various situations.

Professor John Adair, a British academic who is an author of more than forty books on business, military, and other leadership wrote:

"The chief executive who knows his strengths and weaknesses as a leader is likely to be far more effective than the one who remains blind to them. He is also on the road to humility-that priceless attitude of openness to life that can help a manger absorb mistakes, failures, or personal shortcomings."

Practicing mutual respect under all circumstances will allow us to embrace the humility that leads to openness, relationship building, and the ability to navigate the interrelated dimensions of leadership note by SunTzu...the result will be effectively engaging your teams to create sustainable profitable growth.

Chapter 7

All Rise

It was a Thanksgiving holiday and we were celebrating the day at my Grandfather Quinn's apartment in Detroit, Michigan. I was maybe 12 years old. I used to marvel at how large the "apartment" was. In fact, you could probably fit two or three apartments of the size that I was later able to afford when I started work in the early 1970's into his apartment.

There were many rooms, and the "adult" table for Thanksgiving dinner was in a separate room from the room that had the kids' table. Perhaps some of you were relegated to the kids' table at Thanksgiving or other holiday family celebrations. My Grandfather was a kind man who had been successful as an engineer (the building kind, not the train kind) and also larger than life to me. My parents taught me to respect my elders, and that meant several things. When you were among adults you should wait to be addressed, you should never interrupt an adult, and you should rise to greet them when they entered the room. By doing all of these things we showed respect to those who were older and wiser than us. Showing respect in these ways was also a way to influence the judgement of those same adults.

Fast forward to today and we still desire to show respect to those around us; however, it is not as common as it should be to respect another person's point of view through listening longer and truly being present in the conversation. There is also a part of showing respect that comes from the fear of being judged poorly by others.

We don't want the boss to have a negative opinion because she holds judgement over our career. This is what I call the "know your place" theory of respect and was what Dr. Bob Wright, CEO and Co-founder of the Wright Foundation, an organization for leadership, referred to in my interview with him when he said, "Respect is one of the most poorly used concepts in leadership!" When people are intimidated to follow because people in a position to judge them say, "You have to show me respect because of who I am," that respect is not sustainable and neither are the results that are expected from them.

We want the people we have relationships with to feel good about us so that the relationship develops the way we want it to. This is an important understanding of what we have been taught. This is not the same as respect. It can become a case of concentrating on and worrying about judgements by others.

You go into a restaurant and a couple comes in. They might be different than what you are used to seeing in a couple...same gender, different races, different cultures, whatever…as a result, you are consciously or subconsciously staring at them. What if they ask you why you are staring at them? You might think to yourself, "Was I judging them?" The answer is yes in one way or another. Was she pretty? He is not my type? And then what does the next level of judgement mean…what does not my type mean? Because he is a man? Not of my race? What does all this sound like? The thoughts could go on and on and the result could become a negative encounter if we let our thoughts about preference (judgmental thoughts) become judgements. Let's stop the cycle by assuming good will and not assuming the negative intent of judgement until it is explicit. In other words don't assume it is negative on the receiving end just because it is a difference in preference/belief, and don't make it negative on the sending end. Let it go.

Road Rage

Early one morning I found myself running late for a meeting that I was supposed to bring doughnuts for. As I navigated the side streets near my home, I was concentrating on my thoughts for the meeting and was only subconsciously paying attention to the things around me. As I came up the side street and approached the intersection with a busy main street, I stopped at the traffic light preparing to turn right. I thought I noticed that traffic on the busy main street was turning left on to the side street that I was on. The cars seemed to be coming one after another, so in my half aware state I somehow came to the conclusion that they had a left turn arrow and traffic on the busy main road going in the direction I wanted to go had a red light to let those cars turn left. Based on what I thought was happening, I pulled out to turn right. What I didn't realize was that there was no such green arrow for those cars to turn left and no such red light for the cars coming in the direction I wanted to turn! The result was that I inadvertently cut off some traffic by pulling in front of them when I turned right. I received a few honks, but fortunately I did not come close to hitting anyone. I'm sure some folks had to slow down a bit, though.

As I continued on my way, over the next few blocks, several cars that I pulled out in front of passed me. Then one guy in a Jeep Cherokee passed me, eventually changed lanes normally, and was in front of me as we came to a red light ahead. I was going to the store to get doughnuts so I was going to turn left at the light we were approaching. As I put on my turn signal to turn left, the Jeep Cherokee in front of me suddenly put on their left turn signal and cut in front of me into the left turn lane I was getting in.

We both stopped at the red light over the left turn lane. Keep in mind that the lanes going straight still had a green light. When the left turn lane signal turned to a green arrow the Jeep Cherokee stayed stopped in the left turn lane and didn't move to turn at all. Just when the left turn signal was turning to red again, he pulled out into the lanes going straight, which still had a green light, and sped off down the road leaving me stuck at the left turn lane for another cycle of lights. I do not know who the person driving the Jeep was and to my knowledge have never seen that car or person again. I remember that I was frustrated that they blocked my ability to turn. While they were blocking my way, presumably because they thought I had cut them off at the last light when I turned right, I kept thinking there must be a reason I don't know about that they are not turning and I invoked my thought of giving them the benefit of the doubt by showing them respect instead of frustration and anger.

The result was that there was no ugly confrontation that could have escalated into something worse. There was no demonstration of demeaning another person that someone else could have witnessed and perhaps learned the wrong way to act from that experience. Instead, there was a brief disruption to the flow of the day that eventually was handled effectively and without longer-lasting consequences. I was frustrated and even angry after I realized that he was trying to get me stuck at the light. After all, I am human. Realizing where I was on my Emotional Scale, I thought, "How could I respect that person?" I was able to use my trigger word, "Respect," to help me not go up the Emotional Scale to the point of where I would be no longer effective in solving the problem I faced. I was able to meet my initial commitment to the meeting on time, and I avoided creating a destructive relationship with another person. While it is true that I apparently did not create a positive relationship with that person based on my initial actions of turning right on a red light, the door is open to salvaging that relationship if the circumstance occurred because I did not seriously damage it.

That frustration and anger I felt still needed to dissipate over time; however, it dissipated much quicker because of how I was effective in handling where I was on my Emotional Scale at the time and where I could have headed on that scale under a different set of reactions. My "relationship" with that person was strained but not broken, and the result was that the situation was handled without impairing the desired results now or in the future.

Both of us made some form of judgement in the situation. The difference of how the two of us reacted in this situation was the difference between the judgment phase of our brief relationship and the judgmental phase. That difference resulted in each of us ending up on a different level of our Emotional Scale, and that affected our actions and our effectiveness in dealing with a situation we each had unfavorable judgments about.

After all, you don't really know why that person behind you while driving, sped up on your bumper, in an apparent road rage situation. There are a number of emergency situations you may not know. Even in the case of them openly acting like a jerk, you don't actually know the event/events in their life that caused them to go up the Emotional Scale to the point of not acting effectively with others. At the end of the day, when it comes to the relationship side of leadership, it's not about how you feel, it's about the other person's state of mind. The famous Greek philosopher Plato once said, "Be kind, for everyone you meet is fighting a hard battle."

Exercising Demons

How many of you have worked on staying/getting into shape physically? I know I have been on that roller coaster for many rides! So you go into a fitness center that touts itself as being "elite." The place has great reviews online and they have a reputation for their knowledge and process for helping people of all types meet their goals of getting into the best shape possible. They even have the latest interactive technology integrated into their available routines.

With great enthusiasm and some trepidation you take a deep breath, exhale, and walk on in.

You quickly encounter a trainer full of energy and promise to help you achieve your goals. In fact, she describes your goal as "our" goal! You are excited and motivated.

Next, you begin the process of getting into great shape. You then realize that the trainer has set a process that is too aggressive for the condition you are currently in. There is no encouragement on the part of the trainer for you to feel free to give feedback and you agonize in your internal debate about whether to let her know how you feel. In addition, while you struggle to keep up with the program, the trainer is making subtle faces that non-verbally communicate her disdain for your performance.

When you are finally done with that first day of what you thought was going to be the first step to the rest of your improved life, you leave with less enthusiasm than when you arrived. As you lie awake that night waiting to fall asleep, your mind is racing with the dreadful memory of your experience of trying to get into great shape. You feel doubt about your ability to do this and you feel disappointment in your performance based on the trainer's reactions. You are not motivated to try again and you dread your next encounter with the trainer.

Because of how you feel, you are not likely to figure out the best plan to succeed and are not likely to work through the barriers to reaching your goal. Something short of success, if not total failure, to reach your goal will be the result.

As you reflect on the trainer, it may be that based on her frame of reference of being in great shape and working with people in superior shape, she didn't realize that she made her judgments (this may be too hard for the client) about your performance judgmental (making negative faces about your performance). The communication of her judgment in a judgmental form had the effect of putting both of you in a place on your Emotional Scale that was not inductive to creating a relationship that would lead to successfully reaching your common goals.

Daytona 500

In another example, someone peels away from a stop sign at the end of your block and drives with increasing speed by your house while your kids play in the front yard…you can feel the judgement from yourself that the driver is wrong, dangerous, or even a "jerk." However, if you wave your arms, give a stern look, yell at them, or make a gesture with your fingers, you have gone beyond judgement; you are being judgmental.

The nature of the judgement you may make about the risks that are present due to the speeding car can be made based on the relative facts of the potential danger of a car speeding, children, parked cars, and trees nearby.

The nature of the judgmental phase of your feelings and actions are more emotional and are the result of movement along the Emotional Scale described earlier in this book.

From my perspective, the concept of respect has a great deal to do with how we feel about others. It starts with a judgment and then how we feel about that judgment, our judgmental feelings, and influences how we react to that judgment. If we start with realizing how we feel about certain situations, we can better manage our own position on the Emotional Scale by managing the triggers that cause us to move up or down the scale.

How we feel about the situation, excluding the person(s) in it, is one dimension of going from judgment to judgmental. The second dimension involves how we feel about the person(s) we are dealing with. We need to recognize that every human being has at least the same two things in common guaranteed—a heart and a brain. Then we need to realize that anything past that involves judgement about another person, and judgment clouded by emotion becomes judgmental, which can lead to perceived differences. Where we are and where we are going on our Emotional Scale™ at the time of an encounter will many times cause us to react to those perceived differences, resulting in unintended consequences.

Respect in a Crisis

In an interview with Craig Duchossois, Chairman and Chief Executive Officer, The Duchossois Group, he spoke about his beliefs as a leader. His business was originally founded as a supplier of rail cars to the railroad industry. The industry went through deregulation in the late 1980's which sent the industry into a spiral where no one was buying capital equipment. It's important to note his response to this crisis as a leader. He chose to personally visit each of the facilities of his company to explain the situation of the company and what had to be done. This show of respect, to be present and transparent to his associates, built trust in the face of adversity. While on these visits he stated that one person said to him "you owe me a job".

His reply was telling. He replied:

> *"I cannot guarantee everyone a job. As the leader of this business I owe you the very best in terms of the work, environment, benefits, and pay that we can provide"*

Mr. Duchossois' approach demonstrates the respect that people respond to and motivates them to stick together in tough times. People in this type of environment will do their very best in return.

Mr. Duchossios would sustain this respect through communication at "all hands" meetings. These were meetings he held with groups of associates throughout the year on a quarterly basis with all company personnel. In these meetings he demonstrated his personal commitment to transparency as well as a commitment to share his judgments without being defensive or judgmental to those who challenged him. His background was the basis for his leadership style. He came from a military background where he learned how important it is that the soldiers know that, *"as an officer, he had their best interests in mind"*. That learning translated into how and why he listened to the little things that were brought to his attention in the all hands meetings. Sometimes people would ask about providing different sizes of gloves so that people could wear the most effective hand protection. Others would ask for small things that they felt would make their work environment better and more effective. Craig listened to each of these requests and made practical improvements happen for the associates. He believes that this most effectively communicates to the associates *"how much you care and that you have a direct interest in their well-being"*.

Another aspect of Mr. Duchossios' methods of exercising judgment starts with hiring the right people. Over the years he has developed a concept that he calls the *"Cafeteria of personalities with common traits"* which he uses to screen people for his team. Some of the common traits he is looking for are integrity, trust, respect, and share what he described as *"a family value system"*. He explained that he doesn't get upset with a bad business result based on someone's best efforts, however, if associates broke the family value system in their efforts that would be a critical mistake.

Ruling

In my conversation with Dr. Bob Wright, his interpretation of my characteristics of leadership and what I am looking for the reader to take away from this book included:

> *"One of the things you seem to be trying to get to is what I would call availability. You seem to have a vision of the reader finding their own way to be available to other people. So, even if I have hired you to help me, the question is, am I available to be influenced by you, and do I demonstrate that ability?"*

It is one thing to say I am available, my door is always open, but do you really demonstrate that? How do you demonstrate that? Dr. Wright continued:

> *"It will be a different internal experience for each person. So you seem to want to evoke that unique internal experience with each person regarding this concept. I am going to go back to the availability. I define mastery, in this regard as the capacity to recreate the availability concept. We don't always stay available. It's not like I can stay in that space, because I have my own thoughts*

that I recognize – for which I must take responsibility. My own stuff is going to come up, but the question is, am I capable of getting around my own stuff to become accessible and available to you as much as possible...... by taking responsibility to find that internal space of availability, which is the ultimate respect in which I am here to be influenced by you."

This attitude of being available to be influenced will significantly reduce the chances of judgment morphing into a judgmental words or actions.

The way Dr. Wright worded the concept is not the same way I have worded it, however that is the concept. Importantly the other side of it is when you make mistakes trying to create your own space for being available, I want people to realize that it is naturally human and you don't dwell on that and you don't beat yourself up for that. Use the experience to begin to recognize over time when there is enough of a recognizable pattern to learn how to mitigate the mistakes as much as possible. Guilt has no place on either side of the relationship. Letting go of guilt, anger and frustration, will prevent those things from being an influence while going forward, and in turn reduce the chance of judgment or becoming judgmental.

The ability to be good at this is no different than what a sports team or musicians do to perform under the kind of pressure they face in a live performance. How do they get to the point where they can act or react more instinctively than trying to think through everything one step at a time and making mistakes? And the answer is practice. So I am also suggesting that this concept is one that you want to practice to get better over time. It goes hand in hand with the concepts of listening longer and talking with people you don't like in order to practice effective communication in stressful situations without being judgmental.

Dr. Wright commented:

> *"I think that is critical. I would go back to what you said at the beginning I don't believe it is possible to not be judgmental but to take responsibility for my judgments and to be willing to experience the now of another person beyond my judgments and to make my judgments amenable to being tested by my experience ... and so there are a lot of different ways to go about that. One is to share the judgment objectively and allow the person to challenge it in a neutral way."*

He went on to pose the question that is important for leaders to keep in mind:

> *"The question is: do my judgments make me more available or less? Can people talk to me if they have dramatically different perspectives? That prescription to practice talking to people you don't like, that you described, is fantastic. Right now one of the things we are proud of here at the Wright Foundation is that our students are able to engage in what you would call respectful dialogue with people of dramatically different political opinions because they are more personally available to be influenced by others. They don't*

deny their own position but they are interested in understanding other points of view. To be interested is clearly part of that openness and availability."

So again, practicing that means that you have to talk to people in situations where it is not working so you can figure out how to be better and how you can stay available in the moment to use your term.

I heard someone once say "If you are right now you will be right later". In fact, if you are right, it is even more important to take the time to understand others and avoid being judgmental.

Chapter 8

It's Not You, It's Me

Final thoughts on leadership/relationships:

Do you remember a television show that started in 1993 called Seinfeld?

In one episode, the character George Castanza was meeting with his girlfriend Gwen, and she was breaking up with him.

She tells him, "I'm sorry George." He then said, "I don't understand. Things were going so great, what happened? Something must have happened!" To which she explained, "It's not you, it's me." He replied, "You're giving me the 'it's not you it's me routine'? I invented the 'it's not you it's me.' Nobody tells me it's them not me, if it's anybody it's me!" Gwen, giving in, said, "All right, George, it's you." To which George insisted, "You're damn right it's me!"

While the scene is referring to breaking up relationships,

the reality is that in relationships, the most important person is yourself (the "me" in the scene above). The responsibility for the relationship starts with "me." Even though the context of the Seinfeld episode is the ending of a relationship by the false pretense of blaming one's self rather than addressing the issue between the two parties, the fact is that in leadership it is you and not them who has the main responsibility for building the relationship. It starts with you.

Dr. Bob Wright

When I interviewed Dr. Bob Wright, co-founder of the Wright Foundation for the Realization of Human Potential based in Chicago, he initially challenged me on the subject of respect. He said:

> *"I think respect is one of the most misused power and control mechanisms in business that says don't interrupt me and don't be too frisky and don't be too present and don't expect me to have to assert myself with you. I would rather just control you by making you feel guilty for not showing me the respect of letting me finish my sentence so I can dominate. And I have seen that in business since the 70s. I think it is a very misunderstood term that diminishes the quality of relationships tragically."*

He went on to say:

> *"That said, respecting a workforce can*

include wanting them to speak up and it includes getting people with lesser power positions to be heard. So it is not an irrelevant issue, but I think there are more integrative ways to talk about respect."

I pointed out that when I talk about respect, when I think about respect, I don't think about demanding respect from others. I am saying let's think about how we show respect to other people. So it is not an inward thing, it is an outward thing. It's about me, not you.

Dr. Wright made a very good clarifying point: "The way we address what you are referring to is being fully present in the here and now...to be genuine, to be fully present, to be transparent."

We are all influenced by our past experiences. We are influenced by experiences as a child, in school, and the stresses of managing a career. Dr. Wright gives us insight into his journey to develop his leadership skills:

"I was raised by my mother who did not believe in compliments, period. I was only told what was wrong and I was only told once. And she got what she wanted. So for me, I have had to learn to be more positive with people and manage by exception. I throw the job at you and if you mess it up, that is my responsibility. I know I messed it up because I didn't prepare you. So in that sense, I am a pretty decent boss at minimizing the negative. The 1st rule is accentuating the positive and minimizing the negative. Then no one gets more than 50% of

the blame in a situation. When people are trying to prove their point, there is a tendency to try and shoot down the other person's point that doesn't lead to synergistic creative outcomes. You will notice that the usual issue of respect is not articulated here.

I used to try to run my company by consensus. Well that was easy up until about nine employees, but once we got up over nine, it cease being realistic and I have had to grow up a little over the years with a couple different companies. Now I am going to work it through with the employees so that we work it into our strategic plan and they can use the strategic plan as a filter to challenge my arising agendas."

This evolved approach is an example of people understanding that, hey, it is okay to feel the way that you do and how you express it. The added situation that I, as leader, am available to talk about it makes all the difference in how you are being effective with that group. It is not about my agenda, their agenda, or who is going to feel bad about what it is. Respect comes in the sense that we are all here and we are all available. We respect each other's intelligence and ability to do things, and we gather all the ideas for consideration and we filter those ideas by the mutually understood blueprint of a strategic plan.

What I am referring to is the power differential and inclusion of people of lesser power in relationship to people of superior power. And that is really the future.

Dr. Wright's observation is:

"So I think you are positioning this very well because there are levels at which people just verbalizing their opinion is a very big deal. And that gets people engaged. But there are levels at which you earn rights beyond that, so I think what you are trying to get at is how to mobilize the full hearts and minds of people with this respect.

So I want my team to independently own the purpose, mission, and goals of the company, and I want them to be fully engaged so I don't have to mobilize them but they are more like wind in my sails."

His observation is exactly the result of transformational leadership that I want leaders to focus on. As leaders we need to recognize that 75% to 85% of the planet, given various psychology tests, doesn't develop psychologically beyond the desire to conform and, in other words, they spend more of their energy in life avoiding rejection than expressing and being themselves—because it is risky. The "Holy Grail" is the system that has the safety to allow people to express and be themselves and move into a more engaged, meaningful relationship.

To achieve this Holy Grail, it's about the leadership of "me" being present, available, genuine, and fully transparent.

Dr. Wright pointed out:

"That is the kind of the bind that corporations' face where they get lost in bigger

is better. In order for me to really develop everybody in my company, they have to be able to learn and grow and take on new challenges. In order for people to stay, we are going to have to grow as a corporation so that they can take on more challenges in partnership with people who had been ahead of them. And often that gets lost in a growth at all costs attitude rather than what you are trying to get to, which is an integrated developmental game."

Father John

The concept of relationships on the surface may appear for many people to mean that people are getting along all the time, agreeing on issues, and finding solutions problems. Let me clear up that perception. One of the best illustrations of how a relationship works was one in a book titled *Among Friends: Stories from the Journey* by Father John Sichko. He was writing about relationships and respect and his example of relationships was to describe his family when they all get together for dinner. He writes:

"This is how we function. We sit down and pass around the wine. Usually it's my older brother Billy who takes center stage in telling a highlight of the day, story, or joke. We eat and we talk. We talk loudly. We're animated, hands flying up in the air, faces pulled in exaggerated expressions.

Then plates start to fly. And the napkins,

spoons, and forks, too.

That's because we get emotional over what we are conversing about, and we must express ourselves with passion.

And then we bring out the second course, the pasta, and we begin to eat again. We resume talking, but all at the same time, overlapping each other in about eight different conversations. We start getting upset and storm off to our own different parts of the house. Mom brings out the chicken and brings us back to the table. We start talking again and the fight is forgotten.

You see, that's how family really works. Even in the midst of our screaming, talking, and pointing fingers, we understand that this is a part of who we are as a family. If we denied this, we would deny our very selves."

Relationships are built on knowing the other person and allowing respect for each other, or at the very least, our leadership (Mom), to end the escalating commitment to your own point of view so that the relationship can continue effectively even though people in the relationship don't always agree. It helps you to know where you are on the Emotional Scale™ and what triggers your movement up and down that scale. To me, respect is the "mom bringing the family back to the table."

Sue Buchta

Sue Buchta is the CEO of Wilton Brands and has deep

experience in consumer products. Sue is an experienced leader who understands the power of relationships and that respect is the basis for those relationships.

When I asked her about respect in business today, Sue had this to say:

> *"I would say that if you asked me if I feel that there is more respect in business today than there was 10 years ago or less, I would say that there is less. I would definitely say that. I think technology has given people courage or ability—you are not sitting face to face with someone, so tough conversations end up coming across as emails. I would prefer a phone call or a face to face conversation every day of the week, and I think that there are decisions that get made or topics that should be communicated only that way.*
>
> *I would say one of the biggest changes that I have seen is when people hide behind the idea that it is easier for me to just send this email, now I have communicated and I don't have to look at you or awkwardly sit next to you. I don't even really have to answer any questions about it. Even if you email me back I don't have to respond."*

When addressing the attributes a leader should have to set the right culture for performance Sue explained:

> *"Change is a huge challenge. However, if you put people 1st and you respect people even*

*though not everybody is going to agree with you
and not everybody will think that where we are
going and what we are doing is the right thing
and if you are sincere and you are open and
transparent I think that it paves the way to just
a much better culture for performance."*

Robert Jordan

Robert Jordan, as I mentioned earlier in the book, was the anchor journalist at WGN in Chicago for many years. As we discussed the subject of this book, he had a perspective on the effects of technology and the race to disrupt the markets companies compete on the culture of relationships. I found his insights very interesting and an appropriate illustration of the effect that the speed of innovation can have on the culture of respect and sustainable performance of businesses today. He relayed the following analysis of the electronic journalism industry:

> *"I'll give you this example: I was writing a paper, a white paper, for the literary club. During the course of it, I was outlining the history of broadcast paradigm. I had this epiphany while I was writing this.*
>
> *It dawned on me that the technology paradigm shift has halved itself each time it's changed. So film was around for maybe 50 years. Video tape came in, and was around for maybe 12 years. Then we went to digital, which was around for maybe six years, although everything is still digital. But then,*

we went from digital cameras to something called Dejero, which was cell phone cameras..."

(Dejero video transport solutions enable you to reliably reach your global multiscreen audiences instantly and cost effectively. It gives you the power to transport live and recorded video form virtually anywhere.)

"...So instead of shooting microwave to the Handcock and the Sears, now the cameras can shoot cell phone video just like your pocket phone, but it does it in big packs back to the station, and that was around for the last three to four years. Then, for the last year and a half, it's been apps, where we can go live with Periscope or Facebook. Now that paradigm changes almost every six months. Now there are apps that tell you what apps to go find. The paradigm has changed so rapidly that we are no longer able to keep up with it, so businesses, for the 1ˢᵗ time, are encountering this new frontier of changing technology so rapidly that it no longer has the opportunity to become sturdy and reliable.

This disruption is the vogue now, with Uber and other companies that disrupt the way things are going on. So, I'm saying with that understanding, that this paradigm has halved itself to the point now where it's just like, boom, boom, boom, boom, boom, CEO's, business leaders, have to be aware that it's imperative for them to set standards of excellence while they try to keep up with the next, newest, best thing. That's very difficult, because competition is going to try to knock you down again.

Because of this blurry attempt to stay up with changing technology...business leaders, I think, have to find their space, look at this changing, rapidly changing technology, and find their focus and their goals."

Disruption, like that described by Robert, creates stress in operating a business and keeping up with competition. It is a significant contributor to the issues described in the various examples of how relationships work described in this chapter. Timelines to succeed get significantly compressed and the emphasis on short term results and the limit on resources dictated by both of these realities conspire to leave little time for listening longer, engaging all associates with respect, and employing the emphasis on results <u>and</u> relationships. There is also little time for awareness of how we as leaders react to the stressful environments we operate in. The importance of the concepts in this book related to where we are on our Emotional Scale™ and what triggers our movements up and down that scale are more important than ever.

It is our responsibility as leaders to make the time to be aware and work tirelessly to treat our associates with respect. It is the best way to optimize the path of our organizations to succeed in a sustainable way in an environment where the speed of business is very difficult to keep up with.

One last thought: I remember an exchange I had with a

waiter at a restaurant that I had not been to before. The restaurant is known for its great hamburgers. In fact, they have a tremendous menu that lets you build your own version of a hamburger with choices of numerous tasty options. One of the choices is to add onion straws to the burger. I love onion straws...with one caveat...if the batter is not seasoned. I have not acquired a taste for much seasoning, so I asked the waiter if I could have unseasoned onion straws. They offer unseasoned fries and burgers. Based on that he said he thought that was possible.

When the food came to the table I was practically drooling looking at an unseasoned burger and yummy onion straws on top! When I bit into the burger, I suddenly realized that the onion straws had cayenne pepper in them. I made sure I didn't go up on my Emotional Scale™ to the point of ineffective communication, and I calmly called the waiter over and explained that I tasted pepper of some kind in the straws. He apologized and took the burger back to the kitchen to inquire. He returned in a short time with a new burger and said the kitchen explained to him that the batter for the onion straws is made in advance and contains the pepper so it couldn't have been unseasoned after all. He apologized again and I thanked him for taking care of the issue. I said I hope it didn't cause a problem for him. His reply..."that's what I am here for." I call this the "waiter mentality."

That is the right attitude for a leader! It is first and foremost the leader's role to accept responsibility for serving others.

Interviewees for the book

Sue Buchta,
CEO Wilton Inc.

John Cassin,
CEO JDC Solutions

Ashley Joyce,
President The Duchossois Family Foundation

Craig Duchossois,
CEO Duchossois Group

Elliott Greenberg,
CEO JC Licht

Jamie Johnson,
CEO Verde Sustainable Solutions

Robert Jordan,
CEO Jordan enterprises (former anchor WGN)

Steve Kosmalski,
CEO Precious Moments

John Lanman,
CEO Block and CO

Dr. Bob Wright,
Co-Founder and CEO of the Wright Foundation

CPSIA information can be obtained
at www.ICGtesting.com
Printed in the USA
BVHW041123301219
568125BV00013B/299/P

9 781506 906799